THE FAB FOUR COOKBOOK

Rosane Oliveira, PhD

The information provided in this cookbook is for informational purposes only, and is not intended as a substitute for advice from your physician, dietitian, nutritionist, or other health care professional. Always consult with your physician, dietitian, nutritionist, and/or other health care professional before changing your diet and/or beginning an exercise program.

Recipes for Banh Mi Bowl (74), Cocoa-Spiced Quinoa Breakfast Bowl (25), Fluffy Vegan Pancakes (23), Moroccan Tofu (71), Roasted Breakfast Potatoes (26), Tofu Scramble (31), Un-Tuna Sandwich (50), Vegan Shepherd's Pie (63), and Waldorf Salad (72) by Chef Stefen Janke

Design by Tabaruba Design

Photograph on page 62 © Sonja Sarr 2015. Used with permission

ISBN 978-1-7327512-3-1 (paperback)
ISBN 978-1-7327512-4-8 (ebook)

Contents

Introduction

It's time to spice up your plant-based diet!

This cookbook is designed to inspire and motivate you. It is an invitation to explore a plant-based diet, one bite at a time.

The cookbook introduces the concept of the fab four foods and offers a delectable bounty of plant-based recipes in easy-to-follow and quick-to-prepare meals that the whole family will love.

You will learn how to structure your plant-based diet to incorporate the fab four foods and use the principles of energy density every single day.

The Fab Four Cookbook is perfect for you wherever you are on your plant-based journey. Get ready for an experience like no other!

Let's get started!

Before You Begin

The Fab Four Cookbook provides you with a 3-week menu that you can follow as-is or customize as you see fit.

Those who enjoy eating breakfast can start each day by choosing a recipe from the selection provided.

Then, the lunches and dinners are divided into three weeks, each featuring its own international theme around legumes, starchy vegetables, and whole grains:

- **Week 1**
  Latin American Cuisine
  Black Bean, Potato, Quinoa

- **Week 2**
  Mediterranean Cuisine
  Chickpea, Butternut Squash, Wheat
  (with gluten-free swaps)

- **Week 3**
  Asian Cuisine
  Lentil, Soybean, Rice

Between meals, we recommend eating whole fresh fruits and vegetables for snacks and/or desserts.

You may choose to follow each weekly menu as it is presented, or select your favorite options and create a menu that is perfect for your taste and lifestyle.

For example, in the Advanced Prep section on page 82, we suggest recipes that can be scaled up and eaten multiple times throughout the week. We also list the best recipes to prep ahead for easy assembly later on.

SERVING AND PORTION SIZES

All recipes contain 4 to 6 servings, and you can scale them up or down depending on your needs.

When planning your week, remember the difference between serving and portion sizes:

Serving Size
The amount of food that is typically served. For example, a serving of raw leafy green vegetables is one cup while a serving of beans is half a cup.

Portion Size
The amount of food you choose to eat at any one time. That means a portion is 100 percent under your control. You may eat as many servings as you wish in order to create a satiating portion. Every meal can (and should) consist of many servings of different unprocessed and/or minimally processed plant-based foods!

Fab Four

The Fab Four Cookbook was named after the fab four foods of a plant-based diet. They have the highest nutritional value and should be consumed every single day.

Greens

Greens are known for their micronutrients, phytochemicals, and fiber. They include dark leafy greens (like spinach, kale, watercress, beet greens, mustard greens, collard greens, and arugula), and cruciferous vegetables (like broccoli, kale, green cabbage, cauliflower, bok choy, collard greens, and Brussels sprouts).

Beans

Beans are an excellent source of protein and fiber and a good source of folate and other micronutrients. They are classified as 'legumes', which include green beans, fresh peas, soybeans, and peanuts, and 'pulses', which are a subset of the legume family and include lentils and chickpeas.

Berries

Berries are high in phytochemicals that present antioxidant capacity. They include 'horticultural berries' (like strawberries, raspberries, blackberries, blueberries, and açaí berries).

Seeds

Seeds refer to the two most important types of edible seeds, flaxseed, and chia seed, which are rich in omega-3 essential fatty acids and phytochemicals.

The fab four foods are represented in the chart on page 9.

When starting out, make sure to include these four food categories into your daily diet. As you advance on your plant-based lifestyle, keep adding more foods from the other categories listed in the chart.

The Fab Four Cookbook is designed to help you incorporate those foods into your daily diet. Specifically, the menu is filled with recipes featuring different types of beans and greens.

Berries can be added to your breakfast and salads, or enjoyed as a snack or dessert. Ground flaxseed and chia seeds can be added to fruit like papaya, oatmeal, cereals, smoothies, and/or salads.

NOTES

At the bottom of the chart are plant-based foods submitted to different levels of processing. From left to right, they represent increasing energy density.

Fab Four
Greens, Beans, Berries & Seeds

Energy Density
per 100g or 3.5 oz

Berries
1+ Servings

Starchy Vegetables
1+ Servings

Fruits
3+ Servings

31-93 kcal
129-387 kJ

Whole Grains
3+ Servings

71-172 kcal
295-719 kJ

Non-Starchy Vegetables
1+ Servings

55-180 kJ
13-43 kcal

Cruciferous Vegetables
1+ Servings

2,214-2,952 kJ
529-705 kcal

Legumes
3+ Servings

Leafy Vegetables
2+ Servings

Nuts & Seeds
1+ Servings

 **Dairy & Meat Substitutions**	**Grain-Based Foods**	**Sugars**	**Grain-Based Foods** (SOS)	 **Oil-Based Spreads**	 **Oils**
107-400 kcal 448-1,674 kJ	203-388 kcal 849-1,623 kJ	265-397 kcal 1,107-1,600 kJ	472-536 kcal 1,974-2,243 kJ	643-714 kcal 2,690-2,987 kJ	882 kcal 3,690 kJ

Visit ucdim.com/fab-four to download
a copy of the Fab Four Chart.

Energy Density

Energy density is a measure of the amount of energy in a food compared to its weight.

Energy density is represented by kilojoules (kJ) in all countries using the International System of Units, or kilocalories (kcal) in the US.

The energy density of any specific food or recipe varies depending on its ingredients.

The more water and fiber in a food, the lower its energy density, while the more fat in a food, the higher its energy density.

People tend to eat a constant weight of food every day—somewhere between 3-5 pounds, regardless of its energy density.

If you obtain that weight through foods lower in energy density, you will lose weight. Conversely, if you obtain that weight through foods higher in energy density, you will gain weight.

The principle of energy density allows you to reduce your caloric intake without cutting portions.

All you have to do is avoid or substitute high-energy-dense foods with low-energy-dense foods like fruits, vegetables, whole grains, and legumes.

High-energy-dense ingredients are marked with a lightning bolt symbol throughout this cookbook. You can omit these ingredients when they are listed as optional to reduce the energy density of any meal.

The chart on page 9 lists the energy density of different food categories found in a whole food, plant-based diet. It also includes their recommended number of daily servings.

Make sure to use it when planning your meals!

Breakfast

Latin America

	Monday	Lunch	*Quick Quinoa Salad* **34**
		Dinner	*No 'Queso' Dillas* **35**
Whole Fruit **16**			
Whole Grain Bread **18**			
Whole Grain Cereal **19**	**Tuesday**	Lunch	*Creamy Potato Soup* **36**
Homemade Nut Milk **19**		Dinner	*Sweet Potato Nachos* **37**
Avocado Toast With Roasted Chickpeas **20**			
Breakfast Berry-Oatmeal Bake **21**	**Wednesday**	Lunch	*Hummus Veggie Wrap* **38**
Build-Me-Up Breakfast Bowl **22**		Dinner	*Black Bean Chili* **39**
Fluffy Vegan Pancakes **23**	**Thursday**	Lunch	*Golden Beet and Kale Salad* **40**
Oatmeal Muffins **24**		Dinner	*Loaded Potato Skins* **41**
Cocoa-Spiced Quinoa Breakfast Bowl **25**			
Roasted Breakfast Potatoes **26**	**Friday**	Lunch	*Burrito Potato Bowls* **42**
Southwestern Breakfast Burritos **27**		Dinner	*Hummus Veggie Tortilla Pizza* **43**
Sunday Morning Smoked Tofu Benedict **28**	**Saturday**	Lunch	*Lentil Sweet Potato Soup* **44**
Steel-Cut Oatmeal – 4 Ways **30**		Dinner	*Chickpea Cakes and Potato Wedges* **45**
Tofu Scramble **31**			
	Sunday	Lunch	*Black Rice, Mango and Avocado Salad* **46**
		Dinner	*Red Lentil Chili* **47**

Breakfast

Whole Fruit

Whole fruit is a go-to food for plant-based eaters — the ideal nourishment for breakfast as well as for snacks and desserts.

Why is whole fruit such a great breakfast choice?

Low Energy Density: Fruits have an energy density of 140-420 calories per pound. That means you can fill yourself up without the extra calories found in more dense foods.

Nutrient-Rich: Fruits are packed with the essential nutrients your body needs, including vitamins, fiber, and antioxidants.

A serving size of fruit is about 1 cup. Here is how it works out for some popular breakfast fruits:

Apple: 1 small apple, approximately 2 1/4" in diameter.

Banana: 1 large banana, about 8" to 9" long.

Grapes: Approximately 32 seedless grapes.

Orange: 1 large orange, around 3 1/16" in diameter.

Peach: 1 large peach, approximately 2 3/4" in diameter.

Strawberries: About 8 large berries.

Whole Grain Bread

Whole grain bread is also a popular, simple breakfast option for plant-based eaters; however, it should be noted that bread has a higher energy density than fruits, vegetables, and legumes, and it is often topped with spreads that add additional calories.

That said, whole grain bread is an acceptable breakfast, as long as you read the food label carefully before purchasing it at the store.

Make Sure It Is a WHOLE Grain: In the ingredients list, look for words like "whole," "cracked," "stone ground," "sprouted," and "rolled" (example — whole grain flour, cracked wheat, and rolled oats). Avoid words that indicate refined carbs, such as white flour, bleached flour, "enriched," and "fortified."

• Fat: Calories from fat should be less than 20 percent of the total calories; you can calculate this by dividing calories from fat by the calories per serving.

• Sodium: The milligrams of sodium listed on the package should be less than the number of calories per serving.

• Trans Fat: There should be no trans fat in the bread you choose.

• Cholesterol: There should be zero cholesterol listed.

• Added Oils: Avoid added oils or fats including hydrogenated or partially hydrogenated vegetable oils, margarine, shortening, cocoa butter, coconut oil, palm oil, and palm kernel oil.

• Added Sugar: Limit any added sugars among the first 3-5 ingredients on the label, including high fructose corn syrup, sucrose, fructose, evaporated cane juice, agave, molasses, maple syrup, or concentrated fruit juice.

Whole Grain Bread

PREP TIME 5.25 HOURS, COOK TIME 30 MIN, SERVES 12

INGREDIENTS

3 ³/₄ cups pastry flour, whole wheat
1 ¹/₂ cup water, warm
2 tbsp maple syrup ⚡
1 tbsp flaxseed meal ⚡
2 ¹/₄ tsp yeast, fast-acting
2 tbsp rolled oats
2 tbsp sunflower seeds, raw or dry roasted ⚡

DIRECTIONS

1. In a large bowl, combine all ingredients except rolled oats and sunflower seeds and stir until incorporated (dough will be sticky). When too thick to stir, begin kneading by hand, adding additional flour until the dough no longer sticks to the sides of the bowl.
2. Transfer dough into second bowl. Cover and let rise for 2 hours at room temperature then 2 hours in the fridge.
3. Remove dough from fridge. Make a hole in the center and add sunflower seeds and oats. Sprinkle flour on the surface and knead until dough becomes elastic and seeds and oats have been incorporated.
4. Form into a loaf and place in a parchment-lined loaf pan. Cover loosely and let the dough raise 1 hour.
5. Preheat oven to 425°F and place a metal pan on the lowest oven rack.
6. Cut two or three 1/2-inch-deep slashes into the top of the bread.
7. Place bread on upper oven rack, then quickly add 1 cup hot water to the metal pan underneath, then close oven door.
8. Bake 25-35 minutes, or until the dough has risen and is golden brown.
9. Remove from oven and cool 5 minutes in the pan before transferring to a cooling rack. Cool completely before slicing.

Whole Grain Cereal

Whole grain cereal is another breakfast choice for plant-based eaters, but, as with whole grain bread, keep in mind that this option has a higher energy density than fruits and vegetables.

The cereal can be prepared in a plant-based manner by using nut milk instead of regular dairy milk; although, once again, this is a higher energy dense breakfast than whole fruit.

When choosing a dry, whole grain cereal in the store, many of our recommendations for choosing whole grain bread apply.

- Make sure it is a whole grain by looking for words in the ingredient list like whole, cracked, stone ground, sprouted and rolled.

- Choose an option that is high in fiber, which will keep you full until lunch. Between 2 and 3 grams per serving indicates a good source of fiber, while 5 grams or higher is an excellent source.
- Watch out for added sugar. Limit any added sugar among the first 3-5 ingredients. You can always sweeten your cereal at home by adding fresh fruit.

After locating a good store-bought whole grain cereal, it is ideal to make your own nut (or grain) milk because store-bought plant milks may contain unhealthful additives too.

Plus, homemade nut milk is simple to prepare, with only two ingredients! Here is our recipe.

Homemade Nut Milk

PREP TIME 10 MIN, COOK TIME 0 MIN
SERVES 4 CUPS

INGREDIENTS

1 cup nuts, soaked overnight ⚡
4 cups water

DIRECTIONS

1. Place nuts in water to soak overnight, adding 2-3x water to make sure the nuts are submerged and will remain covered even after they increase in volume.
2. In the morning, drain the water out.
3. Add nuts and four cups water to a high speed blender and blend until smooth.
4. Pour liquid into a nut milk bag or cheesecloth fabric to allow to strain. Transfer nut milk into a glass jar. Store it in the refrigerator for up to one week.
5. Shake and serve chilled.

Avocado Toast With Roasted Chickpeas

PREP TIME 5 MIN, COOK TIME 0 MIN, SERVES 4

INGREDIENTS

Roasted Chickpeas (Optional)
4 cups chickpeas, cooked, rinsed
2 tbsp lime juice, freshly squeezed
2 tsp chili powder or smoked paprika
1 tsp garlic powder

Avocado Toast
8 bread slices, whole wheat
4 cups avocado ⚡
¼ cup lemon juice, freshly squeezed
Black pepper, freshly ground, to taste

DIRECTIONS FOR ROASTED CHICKPEAS

1. Preheat oven to 400°F and line baking sheet with parchment paper.
2. Place chickpeas in a bag or bowl. Add seasonings and lime juice and toss to coat.
3. Add to baking sheet and bake until golden brown, about 50 minutes, stirring every 15 minutes.

DIRECTIONS FOR AVOCADO TOAST

1. Toast bread.
2. Add avocado and lemon juice to a bowl. Mash then spread over toast.
3. Top with roasted chickpeas and dressing (optional). Serve.

NOTES

Preparation and cooking time will be longer if Roasted Chickpeas are not pre-made ahead of time.

Suggested Salad Dressing: Lemon Tahini (optional) (page 97)

Breakfast Berry-Oatmeal Bake

PREP TIME 10 MIN, COOK TIME 25 MIN, SERVES 4

INGREDIENTS

2 cups bananas, ripe, mashed
1 cup raisins, yellow or red ⚡
¼ cup walnuts, toasted, chopped ⚡ (optional)
¼ cup pecans, toasted, chopped ⚡ (optional)
¼ cup prunes, dried, pitted, no sugar added, chopped ⚡
2 tsp vanilla extract
2 cups rolled oats
1 cup berries, fresh, halved
¼ cup orange juice, freshly squeezed

DIRECTIONS

1. Mash bananas in a large mixing bowl.
2. Add raisins, walnuts, pecans, prunes, and vanilla extract, then mix.
3. Add oatmeal and stir until well combined.
4. Layer the bottom of a glass baking dish with halved berries, then squeeze fresh orange juice over the berries.
5. Add oatmeal mixture on top.
6. Bake at 350°F for 20-25 minutes and serve while warm.

NOTES

To toast walnuts and pecans, place them on baking sheet and roast at 400°F for 5-8 minutes.

Build-Me-Up Breakfast Bowl

PREP TIME 5 MIN, COOK TIME 50–60 MIN, SERVES 4

INGREDIENTS

2-4 sweet potatoes
1 banana
Cinnamon, to taste
Blueberries (optional)
Chia seeds ⚡ (optional)
Flaxseed ⚡ (optional)
Maple syrup ⚡ (optional)
Nut butter ⚡ (optional)
Nuts ⚡ (optional)
Raisins ⚡ (optional)

DIRECTIONS

1. Preheat oven to 400°F.
2. Poke sweet potatoes several times with fork then bake 50-60 minutes or until fork can easily pierce the center.
3. Mash sweet potato and banana, then mix with cinnamon.
4. Top with desired berries, nuts and seeds. Serve.

Fluffy Vegan Pancakes

PREP TIME 10 MIN, COOK TIME 10 MIN, SERVES 4

INGREDIENTS

½ cup rolled oats
1 ½ cup pastry flour, whole wheat (optional: gluten-free, all-purpose baking mix)
2 tbsp baking powder
2 tbsp flaxseed meal ⚡
1 cup banana, mashed
2 cups Homemade Nut Milk (page 19) or store-bought plant-based milk
2 tbsp maple syrup ⚡ (more to serve)
½ cup blueberries (optional)

DIRECTIONS

1. Add rolled oats to a blender or food processor and blend it until flour.
2. Add whole wheat flour, baking powder, and flaxseed meal to the blender. Pulse to combine.
3. Add bananas, nut milk, maple syrup and mix again.
4. Stir in the blueberries.
5. Heat a non-stick griddle over medium heat.
6. Pour ¼ cup mixture onto heated griddle. Flip to turn over when bubbles start to appear on the surface of each pancake. Cook until brown on both sides. Repeat until all mixture has been used.
7. Enjoy with warm maple syrup.

NOTES

Making this recipe using a high-speed blender will help clean up. In that case, add blueberries to each pancake individually.

Oatmeal Muffins

PREP TIME 15 MIN, COOK TIME 35 MIN, SERVINGS 6

INGREDIENTS

¼ cup Homemade Nut Milk
(page 19) or store-bought
plant-based milk
⅔ cup bananas, ripe, mashed
½ cup apple, grated
1 tsp vanilla extract
1 ¼ cup rolled oats
¼ cup oat flour
1 ½ tsp cinnamon, ground
½ tsp baking powder
¼ tsp baking soda
¼ tsp nutmeg, ground
¼ cup raisins ⚡
¼ cup walnuts, chopped ⚡
(optional)

DIRECTIONS

1. Preheat oven to 350°F.
2. Combine nut milk, bananas, apple, and vanilla in a small bowl.
3. Combine rolled oats, oat flour, cinnamon, baking powder, baking soda, and nutmeg in a second, larger bowl.
4. Transfer wet ingredients into large bowl and mix until combined.
5. Stir in raisins and walnuts (optional).
6. Bake in a standard 12-muffin tin for 35 minutes or until toothpick inserted in the center comes out clean.

Cocoa-Spiced Quinoa Breakfast Bowl

PREP TIME 5 MIN, COOK TIME 30 MIN, SERVES 4

INGREDIENTS

2 cups Homemade Nut Milk
(page 19) or store-bought
plant-based milk
1 cup quinoa
1 cinnamon stick
¼ cup cranberries,
dried ⚡
3 tbsp maple syrup ⚡
2 tbsp cocoa powder,
unsweetened
Ginger, ground, to taste
Nutmeg, ground, to taste

DIRECTIONS

1. Bring nut milk to a low
   simmer. Add all ingredients
   into the milk and reduce
   heat. Cover and cook for
   20-25 minutes.
2. Remove the cinnamon stick.
3. Adjust the thickness by
   adding more nut milk, if
   needed.
4. Garnish with fresh fruit such
   as blueberries, sliced
   bananas, or unsweetened
   shaved coconut.

Roasted Breakfast Potatoes

PREP TIME 15 MIN, COOK TIME 45–60 MIN, SERVES 4

INGREDIENTS

4 cups potatoes, diced
1 cup onion, sliced
1 cup red bell pepper, sliced
1 tsp chili powder
1 tsp dill, dry
1 tsp garlic powder
½ tsp smoked paprika
¼ cup parsley, fresh, chopped

DIRECTIONS

1. Preheat the oven to 375°F.
2. Line a large baking pan with parchment paper or use a silicone baking mat.
3. Rinse the potatoes and scrub dirt off. Cut them in half, then into a large dice.
4. Add to large pot and cover with cold water. Boil for approximately 15 minutes or until just soft.
5. In a sauté pan, add onion and sauté until they turn translucent. Add red bell pepper and continue to cook until onions are caramelized and bell peppers are soft.
6. Drain potatoes and transfer to baking sheet. Add onions, bell pepper, chili powder, dill, garlic powder, and smoked paprika.
7. Roast for 30-40 minutes until crispy and golden.
8. Toss with fresh chopped parsley and extra seasonings, if desired.

Southwestern Breakfast Burritos

PREP TIME 15 MIN, COOK TIME 6-8 HOURS, SERVES 4

INGREDIENTS

1 cup black beans, cooked, rinsed
1 cup tofu, crumbled
½ cup green bell pepper, chopped
½ cup salsa
¼ cup water
2 tbsp green onion, chopped
¼ tsp smoked paprika
¼ tsp turmeric, ground
Black pepper, freshly ground, to taste
Black salt, to taste (optional)
Chili powder, to taste
Cumin, ground, to taste
1 ½ cup spinach
4 tortillas, whole wheat

DIRECTIONS

1. Add all ingredients except spinach to electric pressure cooker. Stir well. Set to Slow Cook on Low setting and cook for 6-8 hours.
2. Add spinach when ready to serve and cook until spinach wilts.
3. Using a slotted spoon, place a scoop of burrito mixture on each tortilla and roll up to seal.

NOTES

This breakfast burrito cooks overnight and is ready to be eaten in the morning. The recipe may also be made quickly on the stovetop. Simply place all ingredients except spinach in a pot and cook (covered with lid) over medium-low heat for 40-45 minutes, stirring occasionally. Add spinach at the end and cook for 5 minutes or until wilted.

Black salt is optional, but it will give the traditional 'egg' taste and smell to the burrito mixture.

Sunday Morning Smoked Tofu Benedict

PREP TIME 3 HOURS, COOK TIME 1 HOUR, SERVES 4

INGREDIENTS

Baked Tofu
2 cups tofu, extra firm, pressed
½ cup water
3 tbsp tamari, low-sodium
2 tbsp maple syrup ⚡
1 tsp liquid smoke, hickory flavor

Hollandaise Sauce
¼ cup white wine, dry
¼ cup brown rice flour
⅛ tsp turmeric, ground
2 tbsp lemon juice, freshly squeezed
1 ½ cup Homemade Nut Milk (page 19) or store-bought plant-based milk
1 tbsp nutritional yeast
1 ½ tsp Dijon mustard

Sautéed Spinach
2 tsp garlic, fresh, minced
4 cups baby spinach, tightly packed
¼ cup white wine, dry

To Serve
4 English muffins, whole wheat
Avocado, sliced ⚡ (optional)
Tomato, sliced (optional)

DIRECTIONS FOR BAKED TOFU

1. Cut pressed tofu into six slabs and place in a container.
2. Mix water, tamari, maple syrup and liquid smoke together.
3. Add liquids to the tofu container.
4. Refrigerate 2 hours (or overnight), flipping tofu in the middle of the time to make sure it is evenly marinated.
5. Preheat oven to 375°F.
6. Line a baking sheet with parchment paper and place tofu on, evenly spaced.
7. Bake for 20 minutes. Flip, then bake for another 15-20 minutes.

DIRECTIONS FOR SAUTÉED SPINACH

1. Place skillet over medium heat. Add garlic and cook until lightly browned, about 2 minutes.
2. Add spinach and toss to wilt.
3. Add wine and cook until it evaporates.

TO SERVE

1. Toast English muffin until golden brown.
2. Place on a plate then top with avocado (optional), tomato (optional), spinach, and tofu.
3. Pour Hollandaise Sauce over top or serve on the side.

DIRECTIONS FOR HOLLANDAISE SAUCE

1. Mix white wine (or water), brown rice flour, and turmeric together (use a small blender to prevent lumps). Pour into a small sauce pan and cook over medium heat for 1-3 minutes.
2. Add lemon juice and cook until sauce has thickened.
3. Add nut milk and stir until smooth.
4. Reduce heat to low and simmer 10 minutes, stirring continuously.
5. Remove from heat and stir in nutritional yeast and Dijon mustard.
6. Pass sauce through a strainer (only if lumps form in the sauce).
7. Keep warm until plating.

NOTES

The long prep time comes from the fact that the tofu should marinate 2 hours before baking. To simplify, the tofu can be marinated overnight, then baked in the morning as you prep and cook the other ingredients, or it can even be prepped days in advance to be used later in the week. Water can be used in place of wine.

Steel-Cut Oatmeal – 4 Ways

PREP TIME 5 MIN, COOK TIME 3 MIN, SERVES 4

INGREDIENTS

Plain Steel-Cut Oatmeal
1 cup steel-cut oats
3 cups water

Version 1: Apple Cinnamon
1 tsp cinnamon, ground
1 cup apple, chopped

Version 2: Banana Nut
1 cup banana, sliced
1 tsp cinnamon, ground
½ cup nuts, chopped ⚡
Maple syrup, to taste ⚡

Version 3: Apple Raisin
½ cup applesauce, unsweetened
1 tsp cinnamon, ground
½ tsp nutmeg, ground
½ cup apple, chopped
½ cup raisins ⚡

Version 4: Chocolate Banana
2 cups banana, mashed
3 tbsp cocoa powder, unsweetened

DIRECTIONS

1. Add steel-cut oats and water to electric pressure cooker. Stir. If preparing Version 1, also add cinnamon and stir. If preparing Version 2, also add banana and cinnamon and stir. If preparing Version 3, also add applesauce, cinnamon and nutmeg and stir. If preparing Version 4, also add 1 cup banana and cocoa powder and stir.

2. Cover electric pressure cooker with lid, close steam vent, choose Manual (Pressure Cook High) and set to 3 minutes.

3. When electric pressure cooker beeps, let the pressure come down naturally in the Warm setting.

4. Let sit about 10 minutes then carefully open lid. Serve in individual bowls. Any additional ingredients listed for each version can be added as a topping to the individual bowls.

NOTES

Steel-cut oatmeal can also be made on the stovetop. Start by boiling water in a saucepan. Next add oats and any ingredients listed in Step 1 for the version you are making. Stir, remove from heat, then cover and store in the refrigerator overnight. Oatmeal can be heated up in the microwave in the morning. Unlike oatmeal made with rolled oats (which become gluey), steel-cut oats get creamier and more delicious when reheated! While we provide four alternative versions, you can also play around by adapting the plain version. Your choice of spices can be added when cooking. When serving, you may stir in nut milk and/or maple syrup, then top with any fresh fruits, nuts or seeds.

Tofu Scramble

PREP TIME 5 MIN, COOK TIME 5 MIN, SERVES 4

INGREDIENTS

4 cups silken tofu, extra firm, lightly pressed
1 tsp turmeric, ground
½ tsp garlic powder
½ tsp onion powder
Hot sauce, to taste

DIRECTIONS

1. Crumble tofu into a non-stick pan, breaking it up with your fingers (a potato masher works well). Add turmeric, garlic powder and onion powder into tofu and mix well. Cook for 2 to 4 minutes or until tofu is hot throughout and most of the liquid has evaporated.
2. Serve with favorite sides and toppings, such as sliced avocado, sliced tomato, salsa, and/or hot sauce.

VARIATIONS

Eat your scramble with veggies for a good energy density balance!

Avocado: Peel, slice, and serve on top of the scramble.

Bell Peppers: Remove stem and seed then finely chop. Cook about 5 minutes then add to tofu mixture.

Potatoes: Recipe for Roasted Breakfast Potatoes is found on page 26. Prepare and then add toward the end of cooking or serve as a side.

Broccoli: Cut about one cup into small florets and then thinly slice the stems. Add along with the tofu.

Carrots: Grate one small carrot and add it toward the end of cooking.

Mushrooms: Thinly slice and add along with the tofu.

Olives: Chop olives and add toward the end of cooking.

Onion: Finely chop one small onion. Cook about 5 minutes (until translucent) then add to tofu mixture.

Spinach: Chop about ½ cup spinach and add toward the end of cooking.

NOTES

For those who cannot eat soy, there are commercial "vegan eggs," which can be used as a substitute for the tofu. There are several brands to choose from, but in general, "vegan eggs" are sold as powder, blended with water, and then cooked like regular eggs.

Latin America

Black Bean
Potato
Quinoa

WEEK 1

Quick Quinoa Salad

PREP TIME 20 MIN, COOK TIME 10 MIN, SERVES 4-6

INGREDIENTS

1 cup tofu, cut into 1/4-inch cubes
1 ½ cup quinoa, cooked
2 cups tomato, chopped
1 cup black beans, cooked, rinsed
½ cup baby lima beans, cooked
¼ cup carrot, chopped
¼ cup green onion, sliced

DIRECTIONS

1. Wrap tofu cubes in paper towels and let stand 5 minutes. Then, in a nonstick pan, heat tofu over medium-high heat until lightly browned, about 10 minutes. Remove from heat and cool.
2. Combine cooked quinoa with dressing of choice and mix well.
3. Add tomatoes, black beans, lima beans, carrots, and green onion. Add tofu and stir gently. Serve.

NOTES
Suggested Salad Dressing: Lemon Basil (page 96)

No 'Queso' Dillas

PREP TIME 5 MIN, COOK TIME 15 MIN, SERVES 4

INGREDIENTS

2 cups potatoes, peeled, chopped
1 cup onion, chopped
2 tsp garlic, fresh, minced
2 tbsp tamari, low-sodium
4 cups spinach
2 tbsp water
Black pepper, freshly ground, to taste
Cayenne pepper, to taste
¼ cup water (from boiled potatoes)
3 tbsp nutritional yeast
8 tortillas, whole wheat
Salsa (optional)
'Queso' ⚡ (page 91) (optional)

DIRECTIONS

1. Boil or steam chopped potatoes, about 10 minutes or until soft. When ready, drain and reserve ¼ cup of the boiling water.
2. Meanwhile, add onions to skillet and sauté over medium heat, adding a few drops of water as needed. Once softened and lightly browned, add garlic, tamari, spinach, and 2 tbsp water. Stir and season with black pepper and cayenne pepper as desired. Sauté until spinach is wilted then set aside.
3. Mash potatoes along with ¼ cup water (used for boiling) and nutritional yeast.
4. Preheat nonstick skillet to medium high heat. Assemble by spreading a layer of potato onto a tortilla then adding sautéed spinach and onions. Top with a second tortilla. Cook on skillet until brown, about 3-5 minutes per side.
5. Serve as-is, or with salsa or 'Queso' (optional).

Creamy Potato Soup

PREP TIME 10 MIN, COOK TIME 20 MIN, SERVES 4

INGREDIENTS

1 cup carrot, peeled, chopped
1 cup celery, chopped
1 cup onion, chopped
2 tsp garlic, fresh, minced
3 cups potatoes, peeled, chopped
2 ⅔ cups vegetable broth, low-sodium
1 cup Homemade Nut Milk (page 19) or store-bought plant-based milk
Black pepper, freshly ground, to taste
Chives (optional)
Green onion (optional)

DIRECTIONS

1. In a saucepan, sauté carrot, celery and onions over medium heat until starting to brown, adding a drop or two of water as needed. Add garlic and cook 1 minute.
2. Add potatoes and vegetable broth. Cover and simmer about 20 minutes until vegetables are tender.
3. Blend with immersion blender in the pot, or transfer and pulse in regular blender.
4. Stir in nut milk and black pepper to taste. Serve as-is or with optional toppings.

NOTES

For a chunkier soup, do not blend completely.

Sweet Potato Nachos

PREP TIME 15 MIN, COOK TIME 30 MIN, SERVES 4

INGREDIENTS

4 sweet potatoes, cut into wedges
Smoked paprika, to taste
2 cups black beans, cooked, rinsed
1 cup salsa (optional)
1 cup sweet yellow corn, roasted (optional)
1 cup tomato, chopped
½ cup cilantro, fresh, chopped (optional)
½ cup green onion, chopped
½ cup Kalamata olives, chopped ⚡ (optional)
Cashew Sour Cream ⚡ (page 90) (optional)
Guacamole ⚡ (optional)
Sunflower seeds ⚡ (optional)

DIRECTIONS

1. Preheat oven to 450°F.
2. Place sweet potato wedges in a single layer on a nonstick baking sheet. Sprinkle with smoked paprika and bake 40-50 minutes, or until soft on the inside and crispy on the outside, flipping half way.
3. Heat black beans.
4. Place wedges on a plate and top with remaining ingredients.

Hummus Veggie Wrap

PREP TIME 5 MIN, COOK TIME 0 MIN, SERVES 4

INGREDIENTS

4 tortillas, whole wheat or brown rice
¾ cup hummus, oil-free
½ cup red bell pepper, cut into thin strips
½ cup cucumber, julienned
Alfalfa or broccoli sprouts (optional)
Avocado ⚡ (optional)
Basil (optional)
Microgreens (optional)
Mint (optional)
Spinach (optional)
Tomato (optional)
8 romaine lettuce leaves, ribs cut away

DIRECTIONS

1. Cook tortillas in a skillet over medium heat for 30 seconds on each side. Tortillas can also be charred directly over the gas flame for a few seconds using tongs. Tortillas can also be warmed in the microwave (covered with a damp paper towel) for 10 seconds to make them more flexible.
2. Spread hummus over each tortilla.
3. Add vegetables (including optional ingredients) to each tortilla. Add lettuce last.
4. Roll each of them up and cut in half or eat whole.

NOTES

A variety of vegetables can be used for the wrap. Remember that moist vegetables will release water and make your wrap soggy. It is fine to use some wetter vegetables (e.g. tomatoes) when combined with other toppings that are drier (e.g. green leafy vegetables, bell peppers).

Black Bean Chili

PREP TIME 10 MIN, COOK TIME 25 MIN, SERVES 4

INGREDIENTS

⅔ cup onion, diced
1 tsp cumin, ground
2 tsp chili powder (optional)
Chipotle powder, to taste
(optional)
1 ⅓ cup vegetable broth,
low-sodium
1 ⅓ cup water
1 ½ cup salsa, chunky
2 cups black beans, cooked,
rinsed
3 cups sweet potato, chopped
into bite-size pieces
½ cup sweet yellow corn
Avocado, sliced ⚡ (optional)
Cilantro, fresh (optional)
Cashew Sour Cream ⚡ (page 90)
(optional)
Green pepper, diced (optional)

DIRECTIONS

1. Start on the chili by adding onions to a large pot. Cook over medium heat until they become soft and translucent.
2. Add cumin and your choice of optional spices and cook for 3 minutes.
3. Add vegetable broth, water, and salsa and increase heat to medium-high. Bring to a boil then reduce heat to medium-low.
4. Add black beans, sweet potato and corn. Cover pot and continue to simmer for 20 minutes.
5. Serve with avocado, fresh cilantro, Cashew Sour Cream, and/or green pepper.

NOTES

For a smoky taste you can add an oil-free plant-based 'bacon' such as seitan or tempeh bacon, or Baked Tofu (page 28) or mushrooms.

Golden Beet and Kale Salad

PREP TIME 20 MIN, COOK TIME 0 MIN, SERVES 4

INGREDIENTS

4 cups kale, thinly sliced
1 ½ cup golden beets, peeled, shredded
1 cup carrots, peeled, shredded
1 cup red bell pepper, diced
1 cup yellow bell pepper, diced
½ cup broccoli sprouts
½ cup green onion, thinly sliced
½ cup hemp seeds ⚡ (optional)

DIRECTIONS

1. Place all ingredients in a large mixing container.
2. Pour dressing over kale mixture and toss until kale is well coated.

NOTES
Massaging the kale for 2 to 3 minutes will make it softer.

Suggested Salad Dressing:
Basil Tahini (page 94)

Loaded Potato Skins

PREP TIME 20 MIN, COOK TIME 70–80 MIN, SERVES 4

INGREDIENTS

6 potatoes
1 cup Homemade Nut Milk
(page 19) or store-bought
plant-based milk
2 tsp garlic, fresh, minced
1 tbsp stone ground mustard
2 cups chickpeas, cooked,
rinsed
6 sun-dried tomatoes, chopped
¼ cup shallot, chopped
3 tbsp capers, cooked
2 tbsp green onion, chopped
Black pepper, freshly ground,
to taste
Tahini Dressing ⚡ (page 103)
(optional)
Baked Tofu (page 28) (optional)
Green onion or chives
(optional)

DIRECTIONS

1. Preheat oven to 400°F.
2. Puncture potatoes several
   times with a fork. Bake on
   baking sheet for about 60
   minutes, or until tender.
   Remove and let cool until
   they can be handled.
3. Cut potatoes in half and
   scoop out the centers.
   Transfer to a bowl and mash
   with nut milk, garlic, and
   mustard. Add chickpeas and
   roughly mash into the
   mixture. Add sun-dried
   tomatoes, shallot, capers,
   green onion and black
   pepper. Stir to combine.
4. Fill potato skins with
   mixture, then continue
   baking 10-20 minutes or
   until golden brown.
5. Serve potato skins with
   toppings of choice

Burrito Potato Bowls

PREP TIME 25 MIN, COOK TIME 45–60 MIN, SERVES 4

INGREDIENTS

4 potatoes
½ cup onions, chopped
½ cup zucchini, chopped
Black pepper, freshly ground, to taste
½ cup quinoa, cooked
½ cup black beans, cooked, rinsed
¼ cup tomatoes, diced, salt-free
2 tbsp cilantro, fresh, chopped
2 tsp lime juice, freshly squeezed
½ tsp chili powder
Red chili flakes, to taste

DIRECTIONS

1. Preheat oven to 400°F.
2. Poke holes in potatoes with fork then cook 45–60 minutes or until a fork pierces through easily.
3. In a nonstick skillet, sauté onions over medium heat until translucent, adding a drop or two of water as needed. Add zucchini and black pepper and cook until soft.
4. Add cooked quinoa and black beans, and cook until heated through.
5. In a bowl, stir to combine all ingredients except potatoes.
6. Cut cooked potatoes in half. Scoop out center and fill with quinoa, bean and veggie mixture. Bake 2-3 minutes.

Hummus Veggie Tortilla Pizza

PREP TIME 20 MIN, COOK TIME 15 MIN, SERVES 4

INGREDIENTS

2 cups hummus, oil-free
1 cup vegetable broth, low-sodium
6 tbsp balsamic vinegar
Black pepper, freshly ground, to taste
1 cup summer squash, thinly sliced lengthwise
1 cup red bell pepper, sliced
1 cup portabella mushroom, sliced
2 cups spinach
4 tortillas, whole wheat or brown rice
Basil, fresh (optional)
½ cup pine nuts or almonds ⚡ (optional)

DIRECTIONS

1. Add 1 cup hummus, vegetable broth, balsamic vinegar, and black pepper to a bowl and stir to make a marinade.
2. Place summer squash, red bell pepper and mushroom slices into the marinade and let sit for 5 to 60 minutes (the longer it sits, the more flavor will be absorbed).
3. Remove vegetables from the marinade and place on a grill pan. Grill a few minutes on each side, until you start to see nice grill marks, then remove from the heat.
4. Lightly steam the spinach then set aside.
5. Place tortillas on a baking sheet and then spread ¼ cup hummus on each.
6. Layer with grilled vegetables, then steamed spinach, then whole leaves of basil (if using), then sprinkle on the pine nuts or almonds (if using).
7. Bake at 375°F for about 15 minutes, or until the edges of the tortilla are a little crispy and the pine nuts/almonds are golden.
8. Sprinkle with freshly ground pepper and serve.

Lentil Sweet Potato Soup

PREP TIME 10 MIN, COOK TIME 16 MIN, SERVES 4

INGREDIENTS

½ cup onion, chopped
½ cup celery, chopped
4 tsp garlic, fresh, minced
1 tsp cumin, ground
1 tsp smoked paprika
½ tsp red pepper flakes
3 ½ cups vegetable broth, low-sodium
3 cups sweet potatoes, cut into 1/2-inch cubes
1 cup green lentils, uncooked
1 cup water
1 ½ cup tomatoes, diced, salt-free
4 cups spinach
Black pepper, freshly ground, to taste

DIRECTIONS

1. Set electric pressure cooker to Sauté. Add onion and celery and cook until softened, about 4 minutes, adding a drop or two of water as needed.

2. Add garlic, cumin, paprika, and red pepper flakes. Stir and cook one minute.

3. Add vegetable broth, sweet potatoes, lentils, water, and tomatoes. Stir.

4. Cover electric pressure cooker with lid, close steam vent, choose Manual (Pressure Cook High) and set to 12 minutes.

5. When electric pressure cooker beeps, let the pressure come down naturally in the Warm setting.

6. Carefully open lid. Add spinach and stir until wilted. Season to taste with black pepper and serve.

NOTES

To make this recipe on the stovetop, follow steps 1-3, then bring to a boil over high heat. Reduce to medium, cover and simmer for 40-45 minutes or until sweet potatoes are tender and lentils are cooked, stirring occasionally. Add spinach and stir until wilted, then serve. The consistency of the soup will differ depending on cooking method.

Chickpea Cakes and Potato Wedges

CHICKPEA CAKES: PREP TIME 10 MIN, COOK TIME 30-40 MIN, SERVES 4
POTATO WEDGES: PREP TIME 5 MIN, COOK TIME 40 MIN, SERVES 4

INGREDIENTS

Chickpea Cakes
1 cup artichoke hearts, rinsed
1 cup chickpeas, cooked, rinsed
1 cup hearts of palms, rinsed
2 tbsp Cashew Cream ⚡ (page 89)
½ cup breadcrumbs
1 ½ tsp Old Bay seasoning
½ tsp Dijon mustard
½ tsp lemon juice, freshly squeezed
Black pepper, freshly ground, to taste
¼ cup breadcrumbs
Tartar Sauce (page 91) (optional)

Potato Wedges
4 potatoes
1 ½ tsp flour, whole wheat or gluten-free
½ tsp chili powder
½ tsp garlic powder
½ tsp onion powder
½ tsp smoked paprika
Black pepper, freshly ground, to taste

DIRECTIONS FOR CHICKPEA CAKES

1. Preheat oven to 400°F and line baking sheet with parchment paper.
2. Pulse artichokes, chickpeas and hearts of palm in food processor until mixed but chunky.
3. Place mixture in bowl. Add Cashew Cream and stir, then combine with ½ cup breadcrumbs, Old Bay seasoning, Dijon mustard, lemon juice, and black pepper.
4. Sprinkle ¼ cup breadcrumbs on a plate. Form mixture into patties then coat each in breadcrumbs.
5. Place on baking sheet. Bake 30-40 minutes, flipping halfway through.
6. Serve Chickpea Cakes with Tartar Sauce (optional).

DIRECTIONS FOR POTATO WEDGES

1. Scrub and slice potatoes into 3/4-inch to 1-inch thick wedges.
2. Steam potatoes in a pot for 15 minutes.
3. Preheat convection oven to 400°F (425°F for regular oven). Line a baking pan with parchment paper.
4. In a large bowl, combine all seasonings and mix. Slowly add steamed potatoes to seasoned mix and coat potatoes evenly.
5. Spread potatoes on parchment paper and bake for 25 minutes.
6. Remove from oven and serve.

NOTES

Store-bought Greek-style plain plant-based yogurt can be used in place of Cashew Cream. You can also use an air fryer.

Black Rice, Mango and Avocado Salad

PREP TIME 70 MIN, COOK TIME 30-40 MIN, SERVES 4

INGREDIENTS

3 cups black rice, cooked
1 cup mango, diced
½ cup onion, diced
½ cup parsley, fresh, chopped
½ cup cilantro, fresh, chopped
(optional)
1 cup avocado, diced ⚡
¼ cup almonds, roasted ⚡
(optional)

DIRECTIONS

1. Combine cooked black rice and salad dressing. Cover and refrigerate about 1 hour.
2. Toss rice with mango, onion, parsley, and cilantro (optional).
3. Scoop into individual salad bowls and top with avocado and almonds (optional).

NOTES
Suggested Salad Dressing:
Cilantro Lime Vinaigrette (page 94)
(double recipe)

Red Lentil Chili

PREP TIME 10 MIN, COOK TIME 10 MIN, SERVES 4-6

INGREDIENTS

2 cups tomatoes, fire-roasted, salt-free
1 cup red bell pepper, chopped
3 tbsp Medjool dates, chopped ⚡
4 tsp garlic, fresh, minced
4 cups water
1 cup red lentils, cleaned, rinsed, uncooked
6 tbsp tomato paste
2 tbsp apple cider vinegar
2 ½ tsp chili powder
2 ½ tsp parsley, dry
1 tsp smoked paprika
¼ tsp chipotle powder
Red pepper flakes, to taste
Avocado ⚡ (optional)
Cashew Sour Cream ⚡ (page 90) (optional)
Herbs, fresh (optional)

DIRECTIONS

1. Blend tomatoes, peppers, dates and garlic in a blender until smooth.
2. Add blended mixture plus all other ingredients (except those listed as optional) to electric pressure cooker.
3. Cover electric pressure cooker with lid, close steam vent, choose Manual (Pressure Cook High) and set to 10 minutes.
4. When electric pressure cooker beeps, let the pressure come down naturally in the Warm setting.
5. Carefully open lid. Serve with your choice of optional ingredients.

NOTES

This recipe can also be made using the Slow Cook function of the electric slow cooker on Low setting for 8 hours or on the stovetop. For the stovetop method, follow Step 1 then add blended mixture plus all ingredients (except those listed as optional) to large pot. Bring to a boil, then reduce heat, cover and simmer until lentils are cooked, about 15-20 minutes.

Mediterranean

Chickpea
Butternut Squash
Wheat (with gluten-free swaps)

WEEK 2

Un-Tuna Sandwich

PREP TIME 10 MIN, COOK TIME 0 MIN, SERVES 4

INGREDIENTS

4 cups chickpeas, cooked, rinsed
½ cup celery, diced
½ cup green onion, sliced
¼ cup Cashew Cream ⚡ (page 89) (more to taste)
¼ cup dill relish
¼ cup red bell peppers, roasted, diced
2 tbsp Dijon mustard
2 tbsp dill, fresh, chopped (or ¼ tsp dill, dry)
2 tbsp lemon juice, freshly squeezed
4 tsp capers, chopped
4 tsp Old Bay seasoning
Black pepper, freshly ground, to taste
Hot sauce, to taste

DIRECTIONS

1. Rinse chickpeas and add them to food processor. Pulse in 15-second bursts, scrape the sides down and repeat until the chickpeas are roughly chopped.
2. Add the chopped chickpeas to a large mixing bowl followed by all remaining ingredients. Mix well.
3. Adjust the moisture of the Un-Tuna mixture by adding more Cashew Cream if desired. Season with freshly ground black pepper and hot sauce to taste.
4. Build into a sandwich using your favorite toppings, e.g. ALT (avocado, lettuce and tomato).

Unlayered Lasagna

PREP TIME 20 MIN, COOK TIME 7 MIN, SERVES 2–4

INGREDIENTS

½ cup onion, chopped
4 tsp garlic, fresh, minced
2 cups water or vegetable broth, low-sodium
1 ¼ cup tomato, diced, salt-free
1 cup tomato purée
¾ cup lasagna sheets, whole wheat, broken
⅓ cup carrots, chopped
⅓ cup red bell pepper, chopped
⅓ cup zucchini, chopped

¼ cup red lentils, uncooked
2 tsp Italian seasoning
¼ tsp garlic powder
¼ tsp onion powder
Black pepper, freshly ground, to taste
Red pepper flakes, to taste
White pepper, to taste
1 tbsp nutritional yeast
1 cup spinach (optional)

DIRECTIONS

1. Set electric pressure cooker to Sauté. Add onion and garlic and cook until softened, about 4 minutes, adding a drop or two of water as needed.
2. Add all other ingredients except spinach and nutritional yeast. Stir well to incorporate everything and to make sure lasagna noodles are dispersed.
3. Cover electric pressure cooker with lid, close steam vent, choose Manual (Pressure Cook High) and set to 3 minutes.
4. When electric pressure cooker beeps, let the pressure come down naturally in the Warm setting.
5. Carefully open lid. Add nutritional yeast and stir. Taste and adjust seasonings as desired. Stir in spinach (if using) and serve.

NOTES

This recipe can also be made on the stovetop. Follow Steps 1–2, then bring pot to a boil, lower heat, cover, and simmer until lasagna noodles are al dente, about 20 minutes. Afterwards, proceed with step 5.

Tuscan Vegetable Soup

PREP TIME 15 MIN, COOK TIME 20 MIN, SERVES 4

INGREDIENTS

½ **cup** carrot, diced
½ **cup** celery, diced
½ **cup** onion, diced
½ **cup** yellow squash, diced
½ **cup** zucchini, diced
2 garlic cloves, pressed
Red pepper flakes, to taste
Thyme, dry, to taste
Rosemary, dry, to taste
3 cups vegetable broth, low-sodium
2 cups cannellini beans, cooked, rinsed
½ **cup** tomato, diced, salt-free
1 ½ cup kale, deveined, chopped
Black pepper, freshly ground, to taste
1 tsp maple syrup ⚡ (optional)
1 ½ tsp white vinegar

DIRECTIONS

1. In Dutch oven or saucepan, sauté carrot, celery, onion, yellow squash and zucchini 4 minutes. Add garlic, red pepper flakes, thyme and rosemary and cook 30 seconds.

2. Add broth, beans and tomatoes and bring to a boil.

3. Reduce heat. Stir in chopped kale. Cover and let simmer 15 minutes.

4. Transfer half of soup to a blender, or use immersion blender to partially purée, leaving some chunks for texture.

5. Add black pepper, maple syrup and vinegar. Adjust seasonings as desired and serve.

Fall Harvest Pasta

PREP TIME 20 MIN, COOK TIME 40 MIN, SERVES 4

INGREDIENTS

2 cups butternut squash, peeled, seeded, diced
2 garlic cloves, fresh, whole
1 cup pasta of choice, uncooked
¾ cup water
¼ cup cashews, raw, soaked overnight ⚡
1 tbsp lemon juice, freshly squeezed
½ tsp onion powder
½ tsp smoked paprika
Hot sauce, to taste
Liquid smoke, to taste

DIRECTIONS

1. Preheat oven to 425°F.
2. Place parchment paper on a baking sheet then add diced butternut squash and whole garlic cloves. Roast 30-40 minutes or until fork tender (squash), flipping half way. Remove from oven and let it cool for 5 minutes. When cooled, pop garlic cloves out of the peel.
3. Meanwhile, cook pasta according to package directions.
4. Transfer squash and garlic to a blender with all remaining ingredients except liquid smoke and hot sauce. Blend.
5. Add liquid smoke and hot sauce (to taste) and blend again.
6. Drain pasta and return to pot. Add desired amount of sauce and stir to combine. Cook until heated then serve.

NOTES

Depending on your preferences, you may have remaining sauce. If so, it can be stored in the refrigerator for up to one week.

Rainbow Pasta Salad

PREP TIME 10 MIN, COOK TIME 10 MIN, SERVES 4

INGREDIENTS

2 cups pasta of choice, cooked
1 cup red bell pepper, chopped
1 cup broccoli, chopped, cooked
1 cup sweet yellow corn
1 cup cucumber, chopped
1 cup onion, chopped
1 cup tomato, chopped
½ cup black olives, sliced ⚡
2 tbsp lemon zest

DIRECTIONS

1. Combine all ingredients in a bowl and toss with dressing of choice. Enjoy immediately or refrigerate to chill.

NOTES
Suggested Salad Dressing: Italian
(page 96)

Portobello and Potato Pot Roast

PREP TIME 20 MIN, COOK TIME 20 MIN, SERVES 4–6

INGREDIENTS

4 cups potatoes, cut into bite-sized pieces
2 ½ cups vegetable broth, low-sodium
2 cups carrots, cut into bite-sized pieces
2 cups pearl onions, frozen
2 cups portobello mushrooms
½ cup red wine, dry
3 tbsp tomato paste
2 tbsp vegan Worcestershire
4 tsp garlic, fresh, minced
1 tsp thyme, fresh
Black pepper, freshly ground, to taste
½ cup vegetable broth, low-sodium
2 tbsp cornstarch

DIRECTIONS

1. Add potatoes, 2 ½ cups vegetable broth, carrots, onions, mushrooms, wine, tomato paste, vegan Worcestershire, garlic, thyme and black pepper to electric pressure cooker. Stir to combine.
2. Cover electric pressure cooker with lid, close steam vent, choose Manual (Pressure Cook High) and set to 20 minutes.
3. When electric pressure cooker beeps, let the pressure come down naturally in the Warm setting.
4. Meanwhile, whisk ½ cup vegetable broth with cornstarch.
5. Carefully open lid. Add cornstarch slurry and stir until thickened, 1-2 minutes. Serve.

NOTES

This recipe can also be made using the Slow Cook function of the electric pressure cooker on Low setting for 6-8 hours or High setting for 3-4 hours. To prepare it on the stovetop, follow Step 1, then simmer covered until potatoes and carrots are soft, about 25-30 minutes, stirring occasionally, then proceed with Steps 4-5.

Fresh Mixed Greens and Berry Salad

PREP TIME 15 MIN, COOK TIME 10 MIN, SERVES 4

INGREDIENTS

½ cup walnuts or pecans, chopped ⚡ (optional)
6 cups spinach and baby greens
1 cup blueberries
1 cup strawberries, sliced

DIRECTIONS

1. If using nuts, preheat oven to 350°F.
2. Toast nuts by placing them on a baking sheet and cooking for about 10 minutes or until fragrant.
3. Remove nuts and allow them to cool.
4. Combine greens, blueberries, strawberries, and nuts in a large bowl.
5. Toss with your choice of dressing.

NOTES

Suggested Salad Dressing: Basic Balsamic (page 93)

Fusilli Alla Puttanesca

PREP TIME 10 MIN, COOK TIME 15 MIN, SERVES 4

INGREDIENTS

½ cup onion, minced
2 tsp garlic, fresh, minced
3 cups vegetable broth, low-sodium
2 cups artichoke hearts, rinsed, chopped
2 cups tomatoes, diced, salt-free
¼ cup Kalamata olives, sliced ⚡
2 tbsp capers
1 tsp basil, dry
½ tsp red pepper flakes
½ tsp thyme, dry
Black pepper, freshly ground, to taste
4 cups pasta of choice, cooked

DIRECTIONS

1. Heat pan on medium-high heat. Add onions and garlic, stirring until golden brown. Add half the broth to pan to loosen onion and garlic and then add remaining ingredients except pasta.
2. Bring ingredients to a boil then reduce heat to medium. Cover the pan and let simmer for 8 to 10 minutes. Add cooked pasta and stir.

Kale Pomegranate Power Salad

PREP TIME 20 MIN, COOK TIME 30-40 MIN, SERVES 4

INGREDIENTS

2 cups butternut squash,
cut into 1-inch cubes
2 tsp garlic, fresh, minced
2 cups Brussel sprouts, halved
2 cups kale, thinly sliced
1 ½ tbsp lemon juice, freshly
squeezed
1 cup chickpeas, cooked, rinsed
1 cup wheat berries, cooked
½ cup pomegranate seeds

DIRECTIONS

1. Preheat oven to 400°F and line a baking sheet with parchment paper.
2. Combine butternut squash and minced garlic. Add to baking sheet and cook 15-20 minutes.
3. Add halved Brussels sprouts to baking sheet with butternut squash. Return to the oven and roast another 15-20 minutes until both are fork tender. Remove and cool 5-10 minutes.
4. In a large bowl, massage lemon juice into kale. Add all other ingredients and toss to combine.

NOTES

Cooked ingredients can be pre-made ahead of time. It is best to wait to combine the ingredients until right before serving.

Suggested Salad Dressing: Lemon Pomegranate (page 97)

Butternut Squash Risotto

PREP TIME 20 MIN, COOK TIME 10 MIN, SERVES 4-6

INGREDIENTS

2 cups butternut squash, peeled, diced
1 cup red bell pepper, diced
½ cup onion, chopped
1 tbsp garlic, fresh, minced
3 ½ cups vegetable broth, low-sodium
1 ½ cup Arborio rice, uncooked
1 cup white mushrooms, chopped
½ cup white wine, dry
½ tsp coriander, ground
¼ tsp oregano, dry
Black pepper, freshly ground, to taste
3 cups greens (e.g., kale, spinach, Swiss chard) (optional)
¼ cup parsley, fresh, chopped
1 ½ tbsp nutritional yeast

DIRECTIONS

1. Set electric pressure cooker to Sauté. Add butternut squash, bell pepper, onion and garlic and cook until starting to brown, about 5 minutes, adding a drop or two of water as needed.
2. Add all other ingredients except greens, parsley and nutritional yeast. Stir well.
3. Cover electric pressure cooker with lid, close steam vent, choose Manual (Pressure Cook High) and set to 5 minutes.
4. When electric pressure cooker beeps, use quick release method to release the pressure.
5. Open lid and add greens (if using), parsley and nutritional yeast. Stir and let sit until thickened, about 5 minutes. Serve.

NOTES

This recipe can also be made on the stovetop. Pre-heat oven to 400°F and roast the butternut squash until it becomes tender and lightly browned, about 25-30 minutes. While squash is in the oven, bring the vegetable broth to a boil on the stovetop and keep it simmering. In a high-sided skillet, sauté onion and garlic on medium-high heat until it starts to soften. Add mushrooms and cook them over medium heat for 5 minutes, then add the red bell pepper and cook for another 2-3 minutes. Add rice and stir for a few minutes until it is toasted. Add white wine and stir until it evaporates. Add hot vegetable broth ½ cup at a time. Continue to stir and add broth as it gets absorbed. The rice should be cooked in 25-30 minutes. Before the last ½ cup broth, add roasted butternut squash and greens (if using). Stir to mix well and add broth one last time. As broth gets absorbed, add nutritional yeast and season the risotto with coriander, oregano and black pepper. Top risotto with parsley and serve immediately.

20-Minute Tomato Soup

PREP TIME 10 MIN, COOK TIME 12 MIN, SERVES 6

INGREDIENTS

1 cup onion, finely chopped
4 tsp garlic, fresh, minced
5 cups water
3 ½ cups tomatoes, crushed, salt-free
½ cup cashews, raw, soaked ⚡
½ cup tomato paste
1 tbsp basil, dry
1 tbsp maple syrup ⚡ (more to taste)
1 tsp oregano, dry
Black pepper, freshly ground, to taste

DIRECTIONS

1. Set electric pressure cooker to Sauté. Add onion and cook until softened, about 4 minutes, adding a drop or two of water as needed.
2. Add garlic. Stir and cook one minute.
3. Add all other ingredients. Stir.
4. Cover electric pressure cooker with lid, close steam vent, choose Manual (Pressure Cook High) and set to 7 minutes.
5. When electric pressure cooker beeps, let the pressure come down naturally in the Warm setting. Carefully open lid.
6. Purée soup using regular or immersion blender. Taste and adjust seasonings and/or maple syrup as desired. Serve.

NOTES

This soup can also be made on the stovetop. Follow steps 1-3 then cook uncovered over medium heat for 20 minutes, stirring occasionally. Finish with step 6.

Shiitake Stroganoff

PREP TIME 15 MIN, COOK TIME 30 MIN, SERVES 4

INGREDIENTS

½ cup shallot, thinly sliced
10 cups mushrooms, fresh, thinly sliced
(e.g. shiitake, oyster, cremini)
2 tbsp flour, whole wheat or gluten-free
1 cup white wine, dry
1 cup vegetable broth, low-sodium
½ cup Cashew Sour Cream ⚡ (page 90)
2 tbsp parsley, fresh, minced (plus more for garnish)
Black pepper, freshly ground, to taste
2 cups wide noodles, egg-free, uncooked

DIRECTIONS

1. In a large saucepan over medium-high heat, add the shallot and sauté until lightly golden, 2 to 3 minutes. Next, add the mushrooms and cook, stirring, until they have softened and released most of their liquid, about 5 minutes.
2. Add the flour and stir to incorporate. Add wine and broth and cook until most of the alcohol has evaporated, about 2 minutes.
3. Remove from the heat, and stir in the Cashew Sour Cream and parsley. Season with pepper.
4. Meanwhile, cook pasta according to the package instructions. Drain, reserving about ½ cup of the cooking water.
5. Add the pasta to the sauce and toss to combine. Warm briefly over low heat to blend the flavors. Add as much of the cooking water as needed to loosen the sauce. Garnish with parsley and serve immediately.

Turkish Chickpea Salad

PREP TIME 15 MIN, COOK TIME 0 MIN, SERVES 4

INGREDIENTS

3 tbsp Dijon mustard
4 tsp red wine vinegar
1 ⅓ tsp garlic, fresh, minced
2 ½ tsp smoked paprika
Black pepper, freshly ground,
to taste
4 cups chickpeas, cooked,
rinsed
1 ⅓ cup Kalamata olives,
rinsed, pitted, sliced ⚡
⅔ cup parsley, fresh, chopped
⅓ cup onion, chopped
¼ cup apricot, dried, chopped ⚡

DIRECTIONS

1. Combine Dijon mustard, red
   wine vinegar, garlic, paprika,
   and freshly ground black
   pepper in a small bowl and
   mix thoroughly.
2. Combine all other ingredients
   in a large mixing bowl.
3. Add the sauce into the large
   bowl and stir until well-
   coated. Serve cold.

Vegan Shepherd's Pie

PREP TIME 30 MIN, COOK TIME 60 MIN, SERVES 4-6

INGREDIENTS

1 cup onion, sliced
4 cups vegetable broth, low-sodium
1 tsp garlic powder
1 tsp onion powder
1 tbsp miso paste, light
1 tbsp vegan Worcestershire
¼ cup tamari, low-sodium
1 tsp rosemary, fresh, chopped
2 ½ tbsp tomato paste
8 cups potatoes, peeled, diced

2 cups butternut squash, diced
1 ½ cup carrots, diced
2 cups green peas
¼ cup cornstarch
¼ cup water
2 cups chickpeas, cooked, rinsed
¼ cup nutritional yeast
¼ cup parsley, fresh, chopped
½ cup Homemade Nut Milk (page 19) or store-bought plant-based milk

DIRECTIONS

1. Preheat oven to 375°F.
2. In a Dutch oven (or large pot), caramelize sliced onion. Remove and roughly chop them. Put onion back in Dutch oven and add vegetable broth, garlic powder, onion powder, miso paste, vegan Worcestershire, tamari, rosemary, and tomato paste and bring to a low simmer.
3. In a separate pot, bring potatoes to a boil. Cook until tender.
4. On a lined baking sheet, roast butternut squash until golden brown.
5. Bring carrots to a boil until just tender (about 3 minutes). Remove carrots and set aside. Keep water. Add peas to boiling water and cook for about 2 minutes. Remove and add to carrots.
6. Combine cornstarch and water to create a slurry. Add slurry to onion mixture.
7. Add carrots, peas, butternut squash and chickpeas to onion mixture. Continue to simmer.
8. For mashed potatoes, strain the boiled potatoes and return to the pot. Add nutritional yeast, chopped parsley and nut milk. Mash until smooth. (Add more nut milk if needed).
9. In a casserole dish, add vegetable mixture. Carefully add mashed potatoes on top until completely covered.
10. Turn on the broiler and cook until potatoes start to turn golden brown on top.

Asian

Lentil
Soybean
Rice

WEEK 3

Mango Fried Rice

FRIED RICE: PREP TIME 30 MIN, COOK TIME 25 MIN, SERVES 4-6

INGREDIENTS

⅔ cup cashews, raw ⚡
1 ½ cup green beans, sliced into 1-inch pieces
1 cup onion, diced
1 tbsp garlic, fresh, minced
1 tbsp ginger, fresh, minced
2 tsp coriander seed, crushed (optional)
Red pepper flakes, to taste
6 cups rice, basmati or brown, cooked, cold

3 tbsp tamari, low-sodium
1 tbsp hot sauce
1 cup tomato, cut into 1/2-inch pieces
2 cups mango, peeled, sliced into 1/2-inch pieces
2 tbsp lime juice, freshly squeezed

DIRECTIONS

1. Preheat a large heavy-bottomed pan over medium heat. Toss in the cashews and dry toast them for about 5 minutes, flipping occasionally until they are slightly browned in some spots. Transfer to a large plate.

2. Turn the heat on the pan up to medium-high. Add the green beans and a scant amount of water. Cook for 3 to 5 minutes, or until the beans are bright green and seared. Transfer beans to the same plate as the cashews.

3. Add onions to the pan and toss for about 3 minutes, or until they are slightly charred but still firm. Add some water if onions begin to stick. Add garlic, ginger, coriander (if using) and red pepper flakes, and toss for 30 seconds or so, being careful not to burn.

4. Add cold, cooked rice and toss to coat. Cook for about 3 minutes, tossing often, until warmed through. Add more water if rice begins to stick.

5. Add tamari, hot sauce and tomato, and toss. Cook for another 3 minutes, or until the rice has browned sufficiently and the tomato is slightly broken down.

6. Add green beans, cashews, mangoes and lime juice. Cook just until mangoes are heated through.

66

Asian-Style Chickpeas

PREP TIME 10 MIN, COOK TIME 3 HOURS, SERVES 4-6

INGREDIENTS

¼ cup tamari, low-sodium
2 tbsp white wine, dry (optional)
2 tbsp balsamic vinegar
2 tbsp maple syrup ⚡
2 tsp garlic, fresh, minced
2 tsp ginger, fresh, minced (optional)
1 tsp red pepper flakes
2 cups chickpeas, cooked, rinsed
1 cup red bell pepper, chopped
½ cup onion, chopped
¼ cup peanuts, roasted, oil-free, salt-free ⚡

DIRECTIONS

1. Add tamari, white wine (if using), balsamic vinegar, maple syrup, garlic, ginger (if using) and red pepper flakes to electric pressure cooker and whisk together.
2. Add chickpeas, bell peppers, and onion and mix until combined.
3. Set electric pressure cooker to Slow Cook function and cook 3 hours on High setting or 6 hours on Low setting.
4. Stir and serve over a bed of rice and top with peanuts.

NOTES

This recipe can also be made on the stovetop. In a small bowl, mix tamari, balsamic vinegar and maple syrup and reserve. Using a nonstick high-sided pan, sauté onion and garlic then add white wine to deglaze it. Add bell pepper and cook until softened. Add chickpeas and cook for 5 minutes. Add reserved tamari mix, ginger, and red pepper flakes. Stir for 2-3 minutes and serve on brown rice.

Veggie-ful Wild Rice Soup

PREP TIME 10 MIN, COOK TIME 60 MIN, SERVES 4

INGREDIENTS

½ **cup** onion, diced
½ **cup** carrot, sliced
½ **cup** red bell pepper, chopped
2 tsp garlic, fresh, minced
½ **cup** mushrooms, sliced
1 cup green beans
1 tsp basil, dry
½ **tsp** oregano, dry
½ **tsp** smoked paprika
Black pepper, freshly ground,
to taste

1 cup tomatoes, diced, salt-free
2 cups vegetable broth, low-sodium
1 cup water
½ **cup** wild rice, uncooked
1 cup white beans, cooked, rinsed
½ **cup** sweet yellow corn
1 cup spinach, chopped

DIRECTIONS

1. In a large saucepan, sauté onion over medium heat for 5-7 minutes until lightly browned.
2. Add carrots and bell pepper and cook for 3 minutes. Add garlic and cook for 1 minute.
3. Add mushrooms, green beans, basil, oregano, paprika, and black pepper. Stir well and cook 3-4 minutes.
4. Add tomatoes, broth, water, and wild rice. Bring to a boil then cover and simmer for 45 minutes.
5. Remove cover. Add white beans, corn and spinach.
6. After spinach has wilted, soup is ready to be served.

Edamame Stir Fry

PREP TIME 10 MIN, COOK TIME 10 MIN, SERVES 4

INGREDIENTS

½ cup tamari, low-sodium
2 tbsp orange juice, freshly squeezed
1 tbsp ginger, fresh, minced
1 tbsp garlic, fresh, minced
2 cups carrots, thinly sliced
1 cup sweet yellow corn
1 cup red bell pepper, chopped
1 cup edamame, shelled
½ cup garlic chives (nira), chopped
Sesame seeds, toasted ⚡ (optional)

DIRECTIONS

1. In a small bowl, prepare sauce by whisking tamari, orange juice, ginger, and garlic. Set aside.
2. In a nonstick skillet over medium heat, add carrots, corn, and red pepper.
3. Cook for 3-5 minutes, stirring regularly and adding a scant amount of water if sticking occurs.
4. Add edamame, garlic chives (nira) and sauce to the skillet. Stir and continue to cook until vegetables are fork tender.
5. Sprinkle with toasted sesame seeds (if desired).
6. Serve as-is or over brown rice or quinoa.

Vietnamese-Style Spring Rolls

PREP TIME 20 MIN, COOK TIME 10 MIN, SERVES 4

INGREDIENTS

2 cups vermicelli or thin rice noodles, cooked
½ cup cucumber, julienned
½ cup red bell pepper, julienned
8 to 10 rice spring roll papers
½ cup mint, fresh, chopped
24 strips Baked Tofu, cut 4-inches long (page 28)

DIRECTIONS

1. To assemble spring rolls, pour warm-hot water into a shallow dish and immerse rice paper to soften for about 10 to 15 seconds.
2. Transfer soft rice paper to a damp cutting board and gently spread out edges.
3. Add mint leaves and julienne strips to the bottom third of the rice paper wrapper, then add a small handful of cooked vermicelli noodles followed by 2 to 3 pieces of Baked Tofu on top. Fold the edges (as if you are making a burrito) and roll the wrapper until seam is sealed.
4. Place seam-side down on a serving platter and cover the spring rolls with a damp warm towel to keep them fresh. Repeat until all 8 to 10 spring rolls are done.
5. Serve them whole or cut them in half or "sushi-style" right before serving.

NOTES

These spring rolls are best when eaten fresh.

For those with soy allergy or sensitivity, replace tofu with mushrooms, non-soy tempeh, or seitan.

Suggested Sauce: Spicy Peanut Sauce (page 107) or Sweet and Spicy Peanut Sauce (page 108)

70

Moroccan Tofu

PREP TIME 10 MIN, COOK TIME 50 MIN, SERVES 4

INGREDIENTS

2 cups tofu, firm, pressed for 10 minutes
2 tbsp miso paste, light
½ tsp garlic powder
1 tsp water
½ tsp cinnamon, ground
½ tsp cumin, ground
½ tsp curry powder
½ tsp smoked paprika
1 cup onion, diced
2 tsp garlic, fresh, minced
4 cups tomatoes, diced, salt-free
½ cup apricots, dried, cut into strips ⚡
½ cup cranberries, dried ⚡
¼ cup tamari, low-sodium
2 tbsp apple cider vinegar
1 tsp dill, dry
2-3 cups couscous, cooked

DIRECTIONS

1. Preheat oven to 400°F.
2. Line a baking sheet with parchment paper.
3. Cut tofu into 6 rectangles and place onto the sheet.
4. Mix miso paste, garlic powder and water together. Spread a thin layer on tofu. Set aside.
5. In a large Dutch oven, gently toast ground cinnamon, cumin, curry, and paprika. Continually stir with a wooden spoon making sure not to burn the spices. Once you smell the aromas of the spices, add onion, minced garlic, tomatoes, dried fruit, tamari, apple cider vinegar and dried dill. Continue to cook over low heat for 40 minutes.
6. At the 25-minute mark, cook tofu in the oven for 15 minutes. The edges should start turning light brown.
7. Place stewed tomatoes (Moroccan Sauce) in bowl then top with tofu.
8. Serve with ½ to ¾ cup cooked couscous per person.

NOTES

For those with soy allergy or sensitivity, replace tofu with mushrooms, non-soy tempeh, or seitan.

Waldorf Salad

PREP TIME 5 MIN, COOK TIME 0 MIN, SERVES 4

INGREDIENTS

4 cups bibb lettuce
2 cups apple, diced
1 cup celery, diced
1 cup grapes, seedless
½ cup parsley, fresh, chopped
½ cup walnuts, roasted ⚡

DIRECTIONS

1. Chop or tear lettuce into a large bowl. Add remaining ingredients.
2. Add dressing to the salad bowl and toss to coat.

NOTES
Suggested Salad Dressing: Smoky Citrus (page 101)

Bulgur and Lentil Pilaf

PREP TIME 15 MIN, COOK TIME 35 MIN, SERVES 4

INGREDIENTS

2/3 cup lentils, uncooked
1 cup leeks, chopped (white and light green parts only)
2 tsp garlic, fresh, minced
1/2 cup bulgur, uncooked
1 tsp cumin, ground
Cayenne pepper, to taste
3 cups water
2 bay leaves
2 1/2 cups leafy green vegetables
(e.g. chard, kale, mustard, spinach) (optional)

DIRECTIONS

1. Transfer lentils to a small saucepan. Add water to cover lentils by at least 2 inches of water.
2. Cook lentils over medium-high heat until almost tender, about 15-20 minutes. If using an electric pressure cooker, cook lentils for 8-10 minutes. Drain and set aside.
3. As lentils are cooking, clean and halve the leeks, then cut them into thin, crosswise slices.
4. Heat a large pot over medium-high heat. Add leeks and cook 5 to 10 minutes until crispy. Set half of them aside for garnishing.
5. Keep half of the leeks in the pot, add garlic and cook for 15 seconds. Add bulgur and cook for 2 minutes, then add cumin and cayenne pepper and cook for 30 seconds.
6. Add water and bay leaves. Bring to a simmer, cover and cook for 15 minutes.
7. Remove bay leaves. If using leafy green vegetables, rinse and add them to the pot, cooking 5 more minutes before serving.
8. Transfer lentil and bulgur to serving dish and top with reserved leeks.

NOTES

This is a versatile recipe that allows a few variations. For example, long-grain rice can be used instead of bulgur, caramelized onions can replace leeks, and the dish can be served with dairy-free plain yogurt.

Banh Mi Bowl

PREP TIME 30 MIN, COOK TIME 10 MIN, SERVES 4

INGREDIENTS

2 cups tofu, extra firm, cut into 4 rectangles
2 cups cabbage, shredded
⅔ cup carrot, shredded
2 cups kale, shredded
2 cups brown rice, cooked
¼ cup radishes, sliced
1 cup cucumber, sliced
1 cup bean sprouts

DIRECTIONS

1. Drain and press tofu for 30 minutes, then rub dressing of choice onto the tofu.
2. Heat a nonstick pan over medium-high heat. Place the tofu in the pan, cooking until it starts to turn light brown. Flip and cook until the other side is light brown as well.
3. Toss the cabbage, carrots and kale with more dressing. Set aside.
4. Build by placing rice in a bowl, then salad on top of the rice. Add tofu to one side of the bowl with sliced radishes next to it, followed by cucumber then sprouts.

NOTES

For those with soy allergy or sensitivity, replace tofu with mushrooms, non-soy tempeh, or seitan.

Suggested Salad Dressing: Sweet and Spicy Asian (page 102)

Teriyaki Rice

PREP TIME 10 MIN, COOK TIME 25 MIN, SERVES 4-6

INGREDIENTS

1 cup carrot, chopped
1 cup celery, chopped
1 cup onion, chopped
1 cup green bell pepper, chopped
1 cup red bell pepper, chopped
2 cups brown rice, uncooked
1 ¾ cup water
⅓ cup tamari, low-sodium
¼ cup maple syrup ⚡
¼ cup rice vinegar
4 tsp garlic, fresh, minced
½ tsp red pepper flakes
1 cup green peas, frozen
Green onion, sliced, to garnish

DIRECTIONS

1. Set electric pressure cooker to Sauté. Add carrots, celery, onion and bell peppers and cook until onions soften, about 4 minutes, adding a drop or two of water as needed.
2. Add all other ingredients except peas and green onion. Stir well to combine.
3. Cover electric pressure cooker with lid, close steam vent, choose Manual (Pressure Cook High) and set to 20 minutes.
4. When electric pressure cooker beeps, let the pressure come down naturally in the Warm setting.
5. Carefully open lid. Add peas, stir, then close lid so they can warm for 2 minutes. Serve garnished with green onion.

NOTES

This recipe can also be made on the stovetop. Follow Steps 1-2 and increase water to 2 cups. Simmer covered over medium-low heat until rice is cooked, about 40 minutes, stirring occasionally, then proceed with Step 5.

Butternut Ginger Soup

PREP TIME 20 MIN, COOK TIME 10 MIN, SERVES 4-6

INGREDIENTS

1 cup onion, diced
1 cup carrot, chopped
4 cups butternut squash, chopped
2 cups water
1 cup apple, chopped
4 tsp garlic, fresh, minced
2 tsp ginger, fresh, chopped
Black pepper, freshly ground, to taste
¼ cup parsley, fresh, finely chopped

DIRECTIONS

1. Set electric pressure cooker to Sauté. Add onion and carrot and cook until softened, about 4 minutes, adding a drop or two of water as needed.
2. Add all other ingredients except parsley and stir.
3. Cover electric pressure cooker with lid, close steam vent, choose Manual (Pressure Cook High) and set to 5 minutes.
4. When electric pressure cooker beeps, let the pressure come down naturally in the Warm setting.
5. Carefully open lid. Purée using regular or immersion blender.
6. Stir in parsley. Taste and adjust seasonings as desired. Serve.

NOTES

This soup can also be made on the stovetop. Follow steps 1-2 then cook uncovered over medium heat for 20 minutes, stirring occasionally. Finish with steps 5-6.

Steamed Vegetable Dumplings

PREP TIME 15 MIN, COOK TIME 17 MIN, SERVES 4-6

INGREDIENTS

1 cup mushrooms, minced
1 ½ cup cabbage, minced
½ cup carrot, shredded
2 tbsp tamari, low-sodium
1 tbsp rice wine vinegar
1 tsp ginger, fresh, grated
12 dumpling wrappers,
round, vegan

DIRECTIONS

1. Set electric pressure cooker to Sauté. Add mushrooms and cook until they release their juices, about 5 minutes, adding a drop or two of water as needed.
2. Add cabbage, carrot, tamari and rice wine vinegar. Stir and cook until liquids have evaporated, about 5 minutes.
3. Add ginger and stir. Remove filling and place in a bowl.
4. Add 1 tablespoon filling to the middle of each dumpling wrapper. Fold in half and press edges together to seal. Repeat for all dumplings.
5. Prepare electric pressure cooker by adding 1 ½ cup water to the bowl and placing a piece of parchment paper cut to fit the steamer. Place dumplings in steamer.
6. Cover electric pressure cooker with lid, choose Steam setting and set to 7 minutes.
7. When electric pressure cooker beeps, use quick release setting to release steam.
8. Carefully open lid. Remove dumplings and serve.

NOTES

This recipe can also be made on the stovetop. Follow Steps 1-4 and then steam using a steamer in a pot with water over the stove for 15-20 minutes.

Tofu and Kale Salad

PREP TIME 100 MIN, COOK TIME 30 MIN, SERVES 2–4

INGREDIENTS

Ginger Garlic Tofu
1 ½ cup tofu, extra firm, pressed
2 tbsp tamari, low-sodium
1 tbsp lemon juice, freshly squeezed
2 tsp garlic, fresh, minced
1 tsp ginger, fresh, grated
¼ tsp hot sauce
½ cup flour, whole wheat or gluten-free

Tofu and Kale Salad
4 cups kale, chopped
1 cup green peas, fresh or frozen
1 cup sweet potatoes, cubed, cooked, cooled
½ cup red bell pepper, chopped
Ginger Garlic Tofu
2 tbsp hemp seeds ⚡

DIRECTIONS FOR GINGER GARLIC TOFU

1. Slice tofu into 1-inch cubes.
2. Mix all other ingredients except flour in a bowl, then add cubed tofu and marinate in the refrigerator for 1 hour.
3. Preheat oven to 350°F and line baking sheet with parchment paper.
4. Lightly coat marinated tofu in flour. Place on baking sheet and bake until golden brown, about 30 minutes. Remove and cool.

DIRECTIONS FOR TOFU AND KALE SALAD

1. Massage kale until it starts to soften and loses some volume, about 5 minutes. Add to a large bowl and toss with dressing of choice. Transfer to individual serving bowls.
2. Arrange peas, sweet potato, bell pepper and Ginger Garlic Tofu on top of kale.
3. Sprinkle with hemp seeds and serve.

NOTES
Suggested Salad Dressing: Lemon Ginger Tahini (page 97)

Tofu Fried Rice

PREP TIME 15 MIN, COOK TIME 60 MIN, SERVES 4

INGREDIENTS

1 cup tofu, extra firm
Sweet Peanut Soy Sauce
(page 108) (double recipe)
1 cup green onion, chopped
½ cup carrots, finely diced
½ cup green peas, fresh
or frozen
4 tsp garlic, fresh, minced
2 cups brown rice, cooked

DIRECTIONS

1. Preheat oven to 400°F and line baking sheet with parchment paper.
2. Squeeze tofu with towel to press out excess liquid then dice into 1/4" cubes.
3. Place on baking sheet and cook 25-30 minutes or until firm and crisp.
4. Prepare a double batch of Sweet Peanut Soy Sauce (page 108).
5. Transfer tofu to sauce bowl and marinate 5 minutes, stirring periodically.
6. Strain tofu out using slotted spoon, reserving remaining sauce.
7. Place tofu on preheated nonstick skillet and cook over medium heat for 5 minutes. Remove and set aside.
8. Add green onion, carrots, peas and garlic to hot skillet. Sauté 3-4 minutes.
9. Add the rice, tofu, and remaining sauce. Cook over medium-high heat for 3-4 minutes, stirring regularly. Serve immediately.

Resources

Advanced Prep

You can download grocery lists for each recipe in this cookbook at ucdim.com/shopping.

Breakfast

If choosing Breakfast Berry-Oatmeal Bake, Oatmeal Muffins, Steel-Cut Oatmeal, or Tofu Scramble, these recipes can be prepared in full on Sunday and enjoyed throughout the week.

If choosing Avocado Toast With Roasted Chickpeas, Roasted Chickpeas can be prepared in advance for easy assembling in the morning.

If choosing Sunday Morning Smoked Tofu Benedict, Baked Tofu can be prepared in advance.

If choosing Build-Me-Up Breakfast Bowl, sweet potatoes can be prepared in advance.

If choosing Southwestern Breakfast Burritos, burrito filling can be cooked overnight so it is ready in the morning.

Cocoa-Spiced Quinoa Breakfast Bowl, Fluffy Vegan Pancakes, and Roasted Breakfast Potatoes are best prepared fresh the day you will be eating them.

Week 1

The following recipes can be made ahead of time and scaled up so you can enjoy them multiple times throughout the week: Black Bean Chili, Creamy Potato Soup, Golden Beet and Kale Salad, Lentil Sweet Potato Soup, Quick Quinoa Salad, and Red Lentil Chili.

Chickpea Cakes can be prepared ahead of time (prepare patties, freeze, then remove from freezer and bake the day you will eat them.)

For any recipe that includes cooked beans, grains, or potatoes, these ingredients can be prepared in advance for easy assembly later on.

Vegetables including bell pepper, carrot, fresh herbs, mushroom, onion, squash, tomato and zucchini can be chopped ahead of time so they are ready to use in recipes.

Dry herbs and seasonings for each recipe can be combined in a bag or container so they are ready to go. Make sure to label each one with the corresponding recipe name.

Suggested dressings and sauces, plus any additional condiments that you choose can be prepared in advance and stored in the refrigerator.

Week 2

The following recipes can be made ahead of time and scaled up so you can enjoy them multiple times throughout the week: 20-Minute Tomato Soup, Fresh Mixed Greens and Berry Salad, Kale Pomegranate Power Salad, Rainbow Pasta Salad, Turkish Chickpea Salad, Tuscan Vegetable Soup, Un-Tuna Sandwich, and Vegan Shepherd's Pie.

The sauces for the Fall Harvest Pasta and Fusilli Alla Puttanesca can be prepared ahead of time, refrigerated, and then warmed up at dinner time, while you prepare the pasta.

For any recipe that includes cooked beans, grains, or potatoes, these ingredients can be prepared in advance for easy assembly later on.

Vegetables including bell pepper, broccoli, Brussel sprouts, carrot, celery, fresh herbs, mushroom, onion, squash, tomato and zucchini can be chopped ahead of time so they are ready to use in recipes.

Dry herbs and seasonings for each recipe can be combined in a bag or container so they are ready to go. Make sure to label each one with the corresponding recipe name.

Suggested dressings and sauces, plus any additional condiments that you choose can be prepared in advance and stored in the refrigerator.

Week 3

The following recipes can be made ahead of time and scaled up so you can enjoy them multiple times throughout the week: Asian-Style Chickpeas, Bulgur and Lentil Pilaf With Leeks (wait to add leafy greens when ready to eat), Butternut Ginger Soup, Mango Fried Rice (wait to add roasted cashews and fresh mango when ready to eat), Moroccan Tofu, Teriyaki Rice, Tofu and Kale Salad, Tofu Fried Rice, Veggie-ful Wild Rice Soup, and Waldorf Salad.

For any recipe that includes cooked beans, grains, or potatoes, these ingredients can be prepared in advance for easy assembly later on.

Vegetables including bell pepper, cabbage, carrot, celery, fresh herbs, green bean, kale, mushroom, onion, radish, spinach, squash, and tomato can be chopped ahead of time so they are ready to use in recipes.

Dry herbs and seasonings for each recipe can be combined in a bag or container so they are ready to go. Make sure to label each one with the corresponding recipe name.

Suggested dressings and sauces, plus any additional condiments that you choose can be prepared in advance and stored in the refrigerator.

Electric Pressure Cooker

Beans

Soaking beans improves their texture and digestion, and it is recommended to include this step when cooking legumes. To accomplish that, place beans in the electric pressure cooker bowl and add four times as much water to account for their expansion while submerged.

Soak beans for 8-12 hours or overnight. Drain the water then rinse beans. Add more water to cover them about two inches (two fingers) above the beans.

Cover the bowl with the electric pressure cooker lid, close steam vent, choose Manual (Pressure Cook High) and set to the time indicated in the chart on page 86. When electric pressure cooker beeps, turn it off and allow the pressure to come down naturally before carefully removing the lid. For red or yellow lentils, use the quick release function.

Grains

Add grains and water according to the ratios in the chart on page 87 and stir to combine. For all grains (except bulgur, which uses the Low setting), select Manual (Pressure Cook High) then set to the time indicated. For most grains, use the quick release function after 2-5 minutes to prevent overcooking. Steel-cut oats require the pressure to fully release naturally.

Potatoes

Whole potatoes should be pricked several times with a fork. Add one cup of water to the bottom of the electric pressure cooker then place potatoes over the metal rack. Select Manual (Pressure Cook High) and set to the time indicated in the chart on page 86. When electric pressure cooker beeps, use the quick release function then carefully remove lid and potatoes.

For cubed potatoes, add water to the bottom of the electric pressure cooker and place the potatoes in the steamer basket. Cover with lid, close steam vent, choose Manual (Pressure Cook High) and set to the time indicated in the chart. When the electric pressure cooker beeps, use the quick release function then carefully remove lid and potatoes.

Stovetop-Oven

Beans

Soaking beans improves their texture and digestion, and it is recommended to include this step when cooking legumes. To accomplish that, place beans in a large bowl and add four times as much water to account for their expansion while submerged.

Soak beans for 8-12 hours or overnight. Drain the water then rinse beans. Transfer to cooking pot and add enough water to cover them about two inches (two fingers) above the beans. Bring beans to a boil for a minute, then keep them at a very gentle simmer for the time indicated in the chart on page 86. The water should barely move.

Simmering beans allows them to cook evenly, retain their shape when tender, and keep their skins intact.

Grains

Add grains and water according to the ratios in the chart on page 87 and stir to combine. Bring to boil then reduce heat to low and simmer covered for the time indicated in the chart. Remove from heat and stir. If there is extra water remaining, cover and let sit 5-10 minutes or until all water has been absorbed then fluff grains with fork before serving.

Potatoes

To bake whole potatoes, preheat oven to 400°F then poke holes in potatoes with fork. Cook for the time indicated in the chart on page 86 or until a fork easily pierces through.

To steam whole or cubed potatoes, add about one-inch of water to a pot. Place potatoes in steamer basket and place steamer basket into the pot. Cover and bring to a boil. When steam starts to escape from lid, reduce heat to a simmer and steam for time indicated in the chart or until the potatoes are soft.

To boil whole or cubed potatoes, place them in a cooking pot then add cold water until it covers the tops of the potatoes. Bring to a boil, then reduce heat, cover and simmer for the time indicated in the chart or until the potatoes are soft.

	Electric Pressure Cooker	Stovetop & Oven
Beans (Soaked)		
Black Beans	6-8	60-90
Black-Eyed Peas	4-5	45-60
Chickpeas	10-15	90-180
Kidney Beans (Red)	7-8	60-90
Kidney Beans (White)	6-9	45-60
Lentils (Beluga)	8-10	20-25
Lentils (Brown, Green)	8-10	20-25
Lentils (Red, Yellow)	1-2	15-20
Lima Beans	6-10	45-60
Navy Beans	7-8	45-60
Pinto Beans	6-9	60-90
Soybeans	18-20	180-240
Potatoes		
Regular, Large, Whole	12-15	45-60
Regular, Small, Whole	8-10	20-25
Regular, Cubed	3-4	15-20
Sweet, Large, Whole	12-15	45-60
Sweet, Small, Whole	8-10	20-25
Sweet, Cubed	2-4	15-20

	Electric Pressure Cooker	Grain:Water Ratio	Stovetop & Oven	Grain:Water Ratio
Grains				
Amaranth	6	1:2	20-25	1:2
Barley (Pearl)	20-25	1:2.5	70-100	1:3
Buckwheat	2-4	1:1.75	15-20	1:2
Bulgur	12	1:2	15-20	1:1.5
Couscous	5	1:1.75	8-10	1:1.5
Farro	10	1:2	65-80	1:3
Millet	10-12	1:1.75	30-40	1:3
Oatmeal	2-3	1:2	12-20	1:3
Oats (Steel-Cut)	3-5	2:3	10-20	1:3
Polenta	7	1:4.5	20	1:4
Quinoa	1	1:1.25	15	1:2
Rice (Arborio)	5-6	1:2	20	1:4 ~ 1:5
Rice (Basmati)	4	1:1	45-55	1:2 ~ 1:2.5
Rice (Brown)	20-22	1:1	45-55	1:2.5
Rice (Jasmine)	4	1:1	15	1:2
Rice (White)	4	1:1	20-30	1:1.5
Rice (Wild)	20-25	1:2	40-60	1:3 ~ 1:4
Teff	2-3	1:2	10-20	1:3 ~ 1:3.5
Wheat Berries	35	1:3	60-90	1:3 ~ 1:4

Condiments

Apple Cider Ketchup

PREP TIME 5 MIN, COOK TIME 0 MIN
SERVES 2-4

INGREDIENTS
3/4 cup tomato paste
2/3 cup apple cider vinegar
1/3 cup water
2 tbsp onion, minced
Black pepper, freshly ground, to taste
2-4 tbsp applesauce

DIRECTIONS
1. Combine tomato paste, apple cider vinegar, water, onion and black pepper in a food processor and blend until smooth.
2. Add 2 tablespoons of applesauce and mix. Taste and adjust applesauce and black pepper to taste.

BBQ Sauce

PREP TIME 5 MIN, COOK TIME 6 MIN
SERVES 4

INGREDIENTS
1/4 cup shallot, minced
1 cup ketchup
1 tbsp apple cider vinegar
1 tbsp maple syrup ⚡
1 tbsp vegan Worcestershire
1 tsp chili powder
1/2 tsp sweet paprika

DIRECTIONS
1. Sauté shallot in a large skillet over medium-high heat until softened, about 3 minutes, adding a drop or two of water as needed.
2. Reduce to low heat. Add ketchup, vinegar, maple syrup, vegan Worcestershire, chili powder and paprika. Stir and cook for 3 minutes.

Cashew Cream

PREP TIME 5 MIN, COOK TIME 6 MIN
SERVES 4

INGREDIENTS
2 cups cashews, raw, soaked ⚡
1 cup Homemade Nut Milk (page 19) or store-bought plant-based milk
2 tbsp miso paste, light

DIRECTIONS
1. Place cashews, miso and nut milk in a blender and blend on high speed until creamy.

Cashew Sour Cream

PREP TIME 5 MIN, COOK TIME 0 MIN
SERVES 2

INGREDIENTS
½ cup cashews, raw, soaked
overnight ⚡
¼ cup water
2 tsp apple cider vinegar
2 tsp lemon juice, freshly
squeezed

DIRECTIONS
1. Add ingredients to high speed
blender and blend until
smooth and creamy. Chill
before serving.

NOTES
If you forget to soak the cashews
overnight (or between 4-8 hours), you
can soak them for one hour in hot
water right before preparing.

Chipotle Mayo

PREP TIME 5 MIN, COOK TIME 0 MIN
SERVES 4

INGREDIENTS
⅔ cup cashews, raw, soaked ⚡
⅔ cup water
¼ cup Medjool dates, chopped ⚡
1 tbsp lemon juice, freshly
squeezed
4 tsp apple cider vinegar
2 tsp Dijon mustard
2 tsp tamari, low-sodium
1 tsp chipotle powder
1 tsp smoked paprika
½ tsp onion powder

DIRECTIONS
1. In blender, blend all
ingredients together until
smooth. Add more water to
reach desired consistency.

Creamy Mayo

PREP TIME 5 MIN, COOK TIME 0 MIN
SERVES 4

INGREDIENTS
½ cup Cashew Cream ⚡
(page 89)
4 tsp hoisin sauce
2 tsp hot sauce
2 tsp maple syrup ⚡
2 tsp tamari, low-sodium

DIRECTIONS
1. Place all ingredients in small
bowl and whisk to combine.
Refrigerate.

NOTES
Store-bought Greek-style plain
plant-based yogurt can be used in
place of Cashew Cream.

Maple Mustard

PREP TIME 5 MIN, COOK TIME 0 MIN
SERVES 2–4

INGREDIENTS
1 tbsp maple syrup ⚡
2 tbsp cashew butter ⚡
1 tbsp Dijon mustard
1–2 tbsp Homemade Nut Milk
(page 19) or store-bought
plant-based milk
Black pepper, freshly ground,
to taste

DIRECTIONS
1. Whisk together maple syrup,
cashew butter and mustard.
Add nut milk to achieve
desired consistency. Add black
pepper to taste.

'Queso'

PREP TIME 5 MIN, COOK TIME 0 MIN
SERVES 2

INGREDIENTS
¼ cup cashews, raw, soaked
overnight ⚡
½ cup salsa
¼ cup red bell pepper, chopped
1 tbsp nutritional yeast
¼ tsp turmeric, ground

DIRECTIONS
1. Drain and rinse cashews.
2. Combine in high-speed
blender with all other
ingredients and blend until
smooth and creamy.
3. Serve warm or at room
temperature.

Tartar Sauce

PREP TIME 5 MIN, COOK TIME 0 MIN
SERVES 2

INGREDIENTS
¼ cup Cashew Cream ⚡
(page 89)
1 ½ tsp sweet pickle relish
½ tsp dill, fresh
½ tsp lemon juice, freshly
squeezed

DIRECTIONS
1. In a small bowl, mix together
all ingredients.

NOTES
Store-bought Greek-style plain
plant-based yogurt can be used in
place of Cashew Cream.

Salad Dressings

Almond Chili

PREP TIME 10 MIN, COOK TIME 0 MIN
SERVES 2

INGREDIENTS
3 tbsp water
2 tbsp almond butter ⚡
1 tbsp lemon juice,
freshly squeezed
1 tbsp maple syrup ⚡
1 tbsp tamari, low-sodium
1 ½ tsp rice vinegar
½ tsp garlic, fresh, minced
¼ tsp serrano pepper, chopped
(optional)

DIRECTIONS
1. Blend all ingredients in a
   small blender or food
   processor until smooth
   and creamy.

Asian

PREP TIME 5 MIN, COOK TIME 0 MIN
SERVES 2

INGREDIENTS
1 tbsp water
1 ½ tsp green onion (green parts), chopped
1 ½ tsp lime juice, freshly squeezed
1 ½ tsp rice wine vinegar
½ tsp maple syrup ⚡
½ tsp tamari, low-sodium
Ginger, fresh, minced, to taste
Turmeric, ground, to taste

DIRECTIONS
1. Add all ingredients to a small mixing bowl and whisk.

Avocado

PREP TIME 5 MIN, COOK TIME 0 MIN
SERVES 2

INGREDIENTS
¼ avocado, ripe ⚡
Lemon or lime juice, freshly squeezed

DIRECTIONS
1. Massage avocado into salad greens before other vegetables are added, then top with a squeeze of lemon or lime.

NOTES
This works best on thicker-textured greens like kale or romaine lettuce.

Basic Balsamic

PREP TIME 5 MIN, COOK TIME 0 MIN
SERVES 2

INGREDIENTS
1 tbsp balsamic vinegar
1 tbsp water
½ tsp Dijon mustard
Garlic powder, to taste
Smoked paprika, to taste

DIRECTIONS
1. Add all ingredients to a small mixing bowl and whisk.

Basil Tahini

PREP TIME 5 MIN, COOK TIME 0 MIN
SERVES 2

INGREDIENTS
¼ cup apple cider vinegar
2 tbsp tamari, low-sodium
2 tbsp tahini ⚡
1 ½ tsp garlic, fresh, minced
½ tsp basil, fresh, chopped

DIRECTIONS
1. Combine vinegar, tamari, tahini, garlic, and basil in a blender and blend until smooth.

Cashew Curry

PREP TIME 5 MIN, COOK TIME 0 MIN
SERVES 2

INGREDIENTS
3 tbsp cashews, raw, unsalted ⚡
3 tbsp water
1 ½ tbsp orange juice, freshly squeezed
½ tsp garlic, fresh, minced
¼ tsp curry powder

DIRECTIONS
1. Place dressing ingredients into a blender and set aside so that cashews can soften.
2. Blend dressing ingredients until smooth. Stir the orange zest into the blended dressing and transfer to a glass container (no additional blending).

Cilantro Lime Vinaigrette

PREP TIME 10 MIN, COOK TIME 0 MIN
SERVES 2

INGREDIENTS
2 tbsp lime juice, freshly squeezed
1 tbsp cilantro, fresh, chopped
½ tsp garlic, fresh, minced
½ tsp maple syrup ⚡
Black pepper, freshly ground, to taste

DIRECTIONS
1. Add ingredients to a food processor and pulse for 15-30 seconds until combined.

Citrus

PREP TIME 5 MIN, COOK TIME 0 MIN
SERVES 2

INGREDIENTS
1 lemon or lime

DIRECTIONS
1. Put a generous squeeze of
fresh lemon or lime juice all
over your salad right before
serving.

NOTES
This method works best on smaller,
individually-served salads.

Fresh Basil

PREP TIME 5 MIN, COOK TIME 0 MIN
SERVES 2

INGREDIENTS
1 ½ tbsp balsamic vinegar
1 ½ tbsp lemon juice, freshly
squeezed
1 tsp garlic, fresh, minced
1 tsp lemon zest
Black pepper, freshly ground, to
taste
2 tbsp basil, fresh, chopped

DIRECTIONS
1. Process balsamic vinegar,
lemon juice, garlic, lemon
zest, and black pepper in a
blender or food processor
until smooth.
2. Add basil and pulse 5 or 6
times until well blended.

Greek

PREP TIME 5 MIN, COOK TIME 0 MIN
SERVES 2

INGREDIENTS
1 tbsp water
1 ½ tsp tahini ⚡
½ tsp Dijon mustard
½ tsp lemon or lime juice,
freshly squeezed

DIRECTIONS
1. Add all ingredients to a small
mixing bowl and whisk.

Italian

PREP TIME 5 MIN, COOK TIME 0 MIN
SERVES 2

INGREDIENTS
2 tbsp basil, fresh, chopped
2 tbsp hummus, oil-free
1 tbsp Dijon mustard
1 tbsp red wine vinegar

DIRECTIONS
1. Add all ingredients to a small mixing bowl and whisk. If needed, add a few teaspoons of water to thin.

Jalapeño Lime

PREP TIME 5 MIN, COOK TIME 0 MIN
SERVES 4-6

INGREDIENTS
2 cups herbs (e.g. cilantro, dill, parsley, mint)
½ cup yogurt, dairy-free ⚡
⅓ cup lime juice, freshly squeezed
2 tbsp jalapeño, chopped, seeded if desired
4 tsp garlic, fresh, chopped
Black pepper, freshly ground, to taste

DIRECTIONS
1. Blend all ingredients in food processor until smooth. Dressing will thicken as it sits and will last up to 1 week in the fridge (the color remains bright green for 3-4 days).

Lemon Basil

PREP TIME 5 MIN, COOK TIME 0 MIN
SERVES 4-6

INGREDIENTS
½ cup basil, fresh, chopped
1 ½ tbsp lemon juice, freshly squeezed
1 tbsp Dijon mustard
1 ½ tsp garlic, fresh, minced
1 tsp lemon zest
¼ tsp maple syrup ⚡
Black pepper, freshly ground, to taste

DIRECTIONS
1. In a small bowl, whisk together all ingredients.

Lemon Ginger Tahini

PREP TIME 5 MIN, COOK TIME 0 MIN
SERVES 2–4

INGREDIENTS
2 tbsp lemon juice, freshly squeezed
2 tbsp tahini ⚡
1 tbsp water
1 tsp ginger, fresh, grated
¼ tsp smoked paprika
Black pepper, freshly ground, to taste

DIRECTIONS
1. In a small bowl, whisk together all ingredients. Add more water to reach desired consistency.

Lemon Pomegranate

PREP TIME 5 MIN, COOK TIME 0 MIN
SERVES 4

INGREDIENTS
1 ½ tbsp lemon juice, freshly squeezed
1 ½ tbsp pomegranate molasses ⚡
1 ½ tsp Dijon mustard
Black pepper, freshly ground, to taste

DIRECTIONS
1. In a small bowl, whisk together all ingredients.

Lemon Tahini

PREP TIME 5 MIN, COOK TIME 0 MIN
SERVES 2

INGREDIENTS
⅓ cup tahini ⚡
⅓ cup water, hot
¼ cup lemon juice, freshly squeezed
1 tsp garlic, fresh, minced
Black pepper, freshly ground, to taste

DIRECTIONS
1. In a small bowl, whisk all ingredients together. If dressing is too thick, thin with additional water.

Low-Fat Italian

PREP TIME 5 MIN, COOK TIME 0 MIN
SERVES 2

INGREDIENTS
1 tbsp apple cider vinegar
1 tbsp water
1/2 tsp Dijon mustard
1/4 tsp agave or maple syrup ⚡
Oregano, dry, to taste
Thyme, dry, to taste

DIRECTIONS
1. Add all ingredients to a small mixing bowl and whisk. Allow to rest 5-10 minutes before adding to your salad.

Maple Tahini

PREP TIME 5 MIN, COOK TIME 0 MIN
SERVES 2

INGREDIENTS
1 tbsp tahini ⚡
1 1/2 tsp apple cider vinegar
1 1/2 tsp maple syrup ⚡
1 1/2 tsp water
1 tsp lemon juice, freshly squeezed
Black pepper, freshly ground, to taste
Cayenne pepper, to taste

DIRECTIONS
1. Whisk all ingredients in a small mixing bowl until smooth and creamy.

Mediterranean

PREP TIME 5 MIN, COOK TIME 0 MIN
SERVES 2

INGREDIENTS
1 tbsp water
1 1/2 tsp hummus, oil-free
1/2 tsp lemon or lime juice, freshly squeezed
1/4 to 1/2 tsp agave or maple syrup. ⚡

DIRECTIONS
1. Add all ingredients to a small mixing bowl and whisk.

Mexican

PREP TIME 0 MIN, COOK TIME 0 MIN
SERVES 2

INGREDIENTS
1 to 1 ½ tbsp of your favorite
salsa

DIRECTIONS
1. Add directly to your salad
   before serving.

Miso Sesame Ginger

PREP TIME 5 MIN, COOK TIME 0 MIN
SERVES 2

INGREDIENTS
¼ cup water, warm
2 tbsp miso paste, light
2 tbsp rice vinegar
2 tbsp tamari, low-sodium
1 tbsp mirin
1 ½ tsp red pepper flakes
(optional)
¼ tsp garlic, fresh, minced
¼ tsp ginger, fresh, minced
Black pepper, freshly ground,
to taste

DIRECTIONS
1. Combine all ingredients in
   blender and pulse until
   smooth.

Mustard Garlic Vinaigrette

PREP TIME 5 MIN, COOK TIME 0 MIN
SERVES 2

INGREDIENTS
2 tbsp Dijon mustard
2 tsp red wine vinegar
1 ¼ tsp smoked paprika
¾ tsp garlic, fresh, minced
Black pepper, freshly ground,
to taste

DIRECTIONS
1. Combine ingredients in a
   small bowl and mix
   thoroughly.

Orange

PREP TIME 5 MIN, COOK TIME 0 MIN
SERVES 2

INGREDIENTS
1 orange, juiced
1 ½ tsp orange zest
1 ½ tsp white wine vinegar
½ tsp Dijon mustard
Black pepper, freshly ground,
to taste

DIRECTIONS
1. Combine orange juice, orange zest, white wine vinegar, and mustard in a bowl and stir well with a whisk.
2. Season with black pepper.

Peanut Ginger

PREP TIME 5 MIN, COOK TIME 0 MIN
SERVES 4

INGREDIENTS
¼ cup peanut butter, roasted, oil-free, salt-free ⚡
3 tbsp tamari, low-sodium
1 tbsp maple syrup ⚡
1 tbsp red wine vinegar
2 tsp ginger, fresh, grated

DIRECTIONS
1. In a small bowl, whisk all ingredients together.

Smoky Citrus

PREP TIME 5 MIN, COOK TIME 0 MIN
SERVES 2

INGREDIENTS
½ lemon, juiced, zested
¼ cup cashews, soaked ⚡
¼ cup water
2 tbsp Medjool dates, pitted, chopped ⚡
2 tbsp silken tofu
1 ½ tsp apple cider vinegar
1 ½ tsp miso paste, light
½ tsp cumin, ground

DIRECTIONS
1. Add all ingredients to a blender and blend until smooth.

Sweet and Spicy Asian

PREP TIME 5 MIN, COOK TIME 0 MIN
SERVES 2

INGREDIENTS
1 to 2 tbsp water
1 tbsp flaxseed meal ⚡
1 tbsp rice wine vinegar
1 tbsp tamari, low-sodium
1 ½ tsp lime juice, freshly squeezed
1 tsp hot sauce
1 tsp maple syrup ⚡
¼ tsp garlic powder
¼ tsp ginger, fresh, minced

DIRECTIONS
1. Mix all ingredients together and allow to sit, giving the flaxseed meal time to hydrate and thicken.

Sweet Citrus Avocado

PREP TIME 5 MIN, COOK TIME 0 MIN
SERVES 4

INGREDIENTS
¾ cup water
½ cup avocado, mashed ⚡
¼ cup lime juice, freshly squeezed
2 tsp maple syrup ⚡
1 tsp garlic, fresh, minced
½ cup cilantro, fresh

DIRECTIONS
1. Place all ingredients except cilantro in the blender and purée until smooth. Stir then add cilantro, pulsing until the leaves break up.

Sweet Raspberry

PREP TIME 5 MIN, COOK TIME 0 MIN
SERVES 2

INGREDIENTS
1 tbsp apple cider vinegar
1 tbsp water
½ to 1 tsp raspberry preserve

DIRECTIONS
1. Add all ingredients to a small mixing bowl and whisk.

Sweet Tahini Ginger

PREP TIME 5 MIN, COOK TIME 0 MIN
SERVES 4

INGREDIENTS
3 tbsp orange juice, freshly squeezed
1 tbsp lime juice, freshly squeezed
1 tbsp maple syrup ⚡
1 tbsp miso paste, light
1 tbsp tahini ⚡
1 ½ tsp ginger, fresh, grated

DIRECTIONS
1. In a small bowl, whisk all ingredients together.

NOTES
To lower the energy density of this dressing, omit the tahini.

Tahini

PREP TIME 5 MIN, COOK TIME 0 MIN
SERVES 2

INGREDIENTS
2 tbsp tahini ⚡
2 tbsp water
1 ½ tsp lemon juice, freshly squeezed (optional)
½ tsp garlic powder (optional)

DIRECTIONS
1. Whisk all ingredients in a small bowl until smooth.

Waldorf

PREP TIME 5 MIN, COOK TIME 0 MIN
SERVES 2

INGREDIENTS
1 lemon, juiced, zested
½ cup cashews, soaked ⚡
½ cup water
⅓ cup silken tofu
2 tbsp Medjool dates, pitted, chopped ⚡
1 tbsp apple cider vinegar
1 tbsp miso paste, light

DIRECTIONS
1. Add all ingredients into a blender and blend until smooth.

Sauces

Chilaquile Sauce

PREP TIME 15 MIN, COOK TIME 20 MIN
SERVES 4-6

INGREDIENTS

½ cup onion, chopped
2 tsp garlic, fresh, minced
3 ½ cups tomatoes, whole,
fire-roasted, salt-free
¼ cup vegetable broth, low-
sodium
1 tbsp chili powder
1 ½ tsp tomato paste
1 tsp cumin, ground
1 tsp hot sauce
¼ tsp oregano, dry
Black pepper, freshly ground,
to taste
Cinnamon, ground, to taste

DIRECTIONS

1. In a nonstick pot, sauté onion
   and garlic until softened,
   about 4 minutes.
2. Transfer onions and garlic to
   blender. Add all other
   ingredients. Blend until
   smooth.
3. Transfer back to pot. Bring to a
   boil over medium-high heat
   then reduce and cook until
   thickened, about 15-20
   minutes, whisking often.

Creamy Lemon Sauce

PREP TIME 5 MIN, COOK TIME 10 MIN
SERVES 2

INGREDIENTS

2 tsp garlic, fresh, minced
3 tbsp flour, whole wheat or gluten-free
2 1/2 cups Homemade Nut Milk (page 19) or store-bought plant-based milk
Black pepper, freshly ground, to taste
1-2 tbsp nutritional yeast (optional)
1/2 lemon, juiced

DIRECTIONS

1. Sauté garlic with a couple drops of water in a nonstick skillet over medium heat.
2. After 1-2 minutes, whisk in flour and cook for 30 seconds then add nut milk and black pepper.
3. Lower heat and allow liquids to thicken, stirring occasionally. If too thin, add an extra tablespoon of flour.
4. When desired consistency is reached, you may add nutritional yeast (optional), then add juice of 1/2 lemon and stir. You may also purée the sauce using a blender.

Enchilada Sauce

PREP TIME 5 MIN, COOK TIME 10 MIN
SERVES 2

INGREDIENTS

2 1/2 tsp flour, whole wheat or gluten-free
3/4 tsp chili powder
1/4 tsp cumin, ground
Garlic powder, to taste
Oregano, dry, to taste
1 1/2 tsp tomato paste
1/4 cup vegetable broth, low-sodium
1/2 tsp apple cider vinegar
Black pepper, freshly ground, to taste

DIRECTIONS

1. In small bowl, measure dry ingredients. Stir and set aside.
2. Place skillet over medium-high heat. When pan has come to temperature, add a few drops of vegetable broth then your spice mixture. Whisk and cook about one minute.
3. Whisk tomato paste into the mixture, then add in vegetable broth. Whisk to remove lumps.
4. Cook for 5-7 minutes or until thickened, whisking regularly.
5. Remove from heat. Stir in apple cider vinegar. Add black pepper to taste.

Garlic Citrus Sauce

PREP TIME 5 MIN, COOK TIME 10 MIN
SERVES 2

INGREDIENTS

1 1/4 cup cauliflower florets, fresh
1/2 cup Homemade Nut Milk (page 19) or store-bought plant-based milk
1/4 cup cashews, raw, soaked overnight ⚡
1 tbsp lemon juice, freshly squeezed
1 1/2 tsp nutritional yeast
Black pepper, freshly ground, to taste
2 tsp garlic, fresh, minced

DIRECTIONS

1. Boil cauliflower florets until very tender, about 7 minutes. Drain.
2. In a high-speed blender, combine cauliflower, nut milk, cashews, lemon juice, nutritional yeast and black pepper. Blend until smooth.
3. In a nonstick skillet, sauté minced garlic until fragrant and soft.
4. Pour in cauliflower sauce and simmer until heated through.

Garlic Dijon Sauce

PREP TIME 5 MIN, COOK TIME 0 MIN
SERVES 2

INGREDIENTS

2 tbsp water or vegetable broth, low-sodium
1 tbsp sherry wine vinegar
1 ½ tsp Dijon mustard
1 tsp garlic, fresh, minced

DIRECTIONS

1. In a small bowl, whisk together all ingredients.

Marinara Sauce

PREP TIME 5 MIN, COOK TIME 20 MIN
SERVES 4

INGREDIENTS

1 cup sweet potato, diced
¼ cup red lentils, cleaned, rinsed, uncooked
2 tsp garlic, fresh, minced
3 ½ cups tomatoes, crushed, salt-free
¾ cup water

DIRECTIONS

1. Set electric pressure cooker to Sauté. Add sweet potato, lentils and garlic and cook until garlic is fragrant, about 2 minutes, adding a drop or two of water as needed.
2. Add crushed tomatoes and water. Stir and cook one minute.
3. Cover electric pressure cooker with lid, close steam vent, choose Manual (Pressure Cook High) and set to 13 minutes.
4. When electric pressure cooker beeps, let the pressure come down naturally in the Warm setting.
5. Carefully open lid. Stir well then purée using regular or immersion blender.

Oil-Free Pesto

PREP TIME 5 MIN, COOK TIME 0 MIN
SERVES 2

INGREDIENTS

1 cup basil, fresh
2 tbsp nutritional yeast
2 tbsp walnuts ⚡
1 ½ tsp lemon juice, freshly squeezed
1 tsp garlic, fresh, minced
¼ cup water
Black pepper, freshly ground, to taste

DIRECTIONS

1. Combine all ingredients except water in a food processor. Blend and then slowly add water until desired consistency is reached. Season with black pepper to taste.

NOTES FOR MARINARA SAUCE

This recipe can also be made on the stovetop. Follow Steps 1-2, then bring pot to a boil, reduce heat, cover, and simmer until lentils are cooked and sweet potatoes are soft, about 25-30 minutes. Afterwards, proceed with Step 6.

Pomodoro Sauce

PREP TIME 5 MIN, COOK TIME 10 MIN
SERVES 2

INGREDIENTS

½ cup onion, chopped
2 tsp garlic, fresh, minced
1 cup tomatoes, diced, salt-free
¾ cup vegetable broth, low-sodium
1 tbsp balsamic vinegar
2 tbsp basil, fresh, chopped
Red pepper flakes, to taste
Black pepper, freshly ground, to taste

DIRECTIONS

1. Heat a deep skillet over medium-high heat and sauté onions and garlic until lightly brown and translucent, adding a drop of vegetable broth if sticking occurs.
2. Add tomatoes, broth and balsamic vinegar and simmer for about 8 minutes.
3. Stir in basil, red pepper flakes and black pepper. Taste and adjust seasoning as needed.

Roasted Butternut Squash Sauce

PREP TIME 10 MIN, COOK TIME 40 MIN
SERVES 2

INGREDIENTS

1 cup butternut squash, peeled, seeded, diced
1 garlic clove, fresh, whole
6 tbsp water
2 tbsp cashews, raw, soaked overnight ⚡
1 ½ tsp lemon juice, freshly squeezed
¼ tsp onion powder
¼ tsp smoked paprika
Hot sauce, to taste
Liquid smoke, to taste

DIRECTIONS

1. Preheat oven to 425°F.
2. Place parchment paper on a baking sheet then add diced butternut squash and whole garlic clove. Roast 30-40 minutes or until fork tender (squash), flipping half way. Remove from oven and let it cool for 5 minutes. When cooled, pop garlic clove out of the peel.
3. Transfer squash and garlic to a blender with all remaining ingredients except hot sauce and liquid smoke. Blend until smooth.
4. Add hot sauce and liquid smoke (to taste) and blend again.

Spicy Peanut Sauce

PREP TIME 10 MIN, COOK TIME 15 MIN
SERVES 2

INGREDIENTS

¼ cup peanut butter, roasted, oil-free, salt-free ⚡
3 tbsp tamari, low-sodium
¾ tbsp hot sauce
1 ½ tsp sesame seeds, toasted ⚡
Water, hot

DIRECTIONS

1. Whisk together all ingredients. If too thick, thin with hot water.

Sweet and Spicy Peanut Sauce

PREP TIME 5 MIN, COOK TIME 0 MIN
SERVES 4

INGREDIENTS
½ cup peanut butter, roasted, oil-free, salt-free ⚡
2-3 tbsp maple syrup ⚡
1 ½ tbsp tamari, low-sodium
1 tbsp lime juice, freshly squeezed
¼ tsp red pepper flakes
Water, hot

DIRECTIONS
1. Make sauce by whisking together all ingredients in a bowl then adding hot water to thin to desired consistency.

Sweet Peanut Soy Sauce

PREP TIME 5 MIN, COOK TIME 0 MIN
SERVES 2

INGREDIENTS
3 tbsp tamari, low-sodium
2 tbsp maple syrup ⚡
1 tbsp peanut butter, roasted, oil-free, salt-free ⚡
1 tsp garlic, fresh, minced
½ to 1 tsp chili powder

DIRECTIONS
1. In a bowl, whisk all ingredients together and set aside.

Sweet Soy Sauce

PREP TIME 5 MIN, COOK TIME 0 MIN
SERVES 2

INGREDIENTS
1 ½ tsp rice vinegar
1 ½ tsp tamari, low-sodium
1 tbsp agave or maple syrup ⚡

DIRECTIONS
1. Mix ingredients together in a small bowl.

Teriyaki Sauce

PREP TIME 5 MIN, COOK TIME 0 MIN
SERVES 2

INGREDIENTS
1 1/2 tbsp rice vinegar
1 1/2 tbsp tamari, low-sodium
1 1/2 tsp agave or maple syrup ⚡
1 tsp garlic, fresh, minced
3/4 tsp ginger, fresh, minced
1/2 tsp cornstarch
1/4 tsp red pepper flakes
Black pepper, freshly ground,
to taste

DIRECTIONS
1. In a small bowl, whisk
together ingredients.

Thai Chili Sauce

PREP TIME 5 MIN, COOK TIME 0 MIN
SERVES 2

INGREDIENTS
1/2 red chili, dried
2 tbsp lime juice, freshly
squeezed
2 tbsp tamari, low-sodium
1 1/2 tsp garlic, fresh, minced

DIRECTIONS
1. Pulse all ingredients in food
processor until combined.
Taste and add additional dried
red chili if desired.

Vegan Cream Sauce

PREP TIME 5 MIN, COOK TIME 0 MIN
SERVES 2

INGREDIENTS
1/2 cup Homemade Nut Milk
(page 19) or store-bought
plant-based milk
3 tbsp nutritional yeast
1 1/2 tsp cornstarch
1 tsp tahini ⚡ (optional)
1/2 tsp lemon juice, freshly
squeezed
1/4 tsp onion powder
Black pepper, freshly ground,
to taste
Cayenne pepper, to taste

DIRECTIONS
1. Blend all ingredients until
smooth.

Index

Author

Rosane Oliveira, PhD is Founding Director of the Integrative Medicine program and Adjunct Assistant Professor of Public Health Sciences at the School of Medicine at the University of California Davis.

She has over 20 years of experience in genetic research with a special interest in nutritional genomics, which explores how diet can turn genes on and off and influence both health and longevity.

Every year in November, Dr. Oliveira coaches tens of thousands of people around the world on how to successfully adopt a whole food, plant-based lifestyle by hosting a 21-day plant-based challenge.

She is the creator of Bite-Sized, a program designed to help people implement lasting habit change. She also writes about health and nutrition on the program's popular blog and teaches lifestyle medicine to medical students at UC Davis.

Let's Connect!

The Fab Four Cookbook has been designed to provide structure, guidance, and recipes for three weeks to make starting or resetting a plant-based lifestyle easy, delicious, and fun.

You can continue to receive on-going support from us by visiting ucdim.com/amazon to sign up for our weekly videos and plant-based recipes!

You can also connect with us on social media by following @drrosane and @ucdim on Facebook, Twitter and Instagram.

Made in the USA
San Bernardino,
CA